LITERATURE FOR VOICE

*An Index of Songs in Collections
and Source Book for Teachers of Singing*

by
Thomas Goleeke

The Scarecrow Press, Inc.
Metuchen, N.J., and London
1984

Library of Congress Cataloging in Publication Data

Goleeke, Thomas
    Literature for voice.

    Includes indexes.
    Bibliography: p.
    Discography: p.
    1. Songs--Indexes. 2. Singing--Instruction and study.
I. Title.
ML128.S3G64 1984   016.7843   84-5461
ISBN 0-8108-1702-0

This book is lovingly dedicated to my children Sherral, Glenn and Sharon.

Preface

This book had its beginnings many years ago, when, as a young first-
year teacher, I suddenly realized I knew little about available repertoire
for beginning students. After years of collecting material and information,
I started organizing, and thanks to a Sabbatical leave from the University
of Puget Sound, was able to complete the work.

What follows is an index of over 60 collections and class voice anthologies, all of which are currently in print and available. Each entry shows
a song's range in musical notation. It then becomes a simple matter to
determine whether a particular volume is suited to a particular student, or
where to find a specific song.

The careful reader will notice I did not index any sacred collections,
collections of arias or duets. Maybe they will become volume 2.

The bibliographies are meant to be used as a point of reference for
one's personal library, school library, and in pedagogy classes.

Also, I thought it would be helpful to present the available audio
material. It seems to be so much more convenient having it all together.

It is my earnest hope that this book will be useful and practical. If
it is, my time will have been well spent.

My thanks to the University, Peggy Smith (of Spokane's Sampson-Ayers
House of Music) and my typist, Ann Jacobson.

CONTENTS

PART ONE

AN INDEX OF SONGS IN COLLECTIONS

PART TWO

IMPORTANT SOURCE MATERIAL

FUNCTIONAL LESSONS IN SINGING, SECOND EDITION

By Ivan Trusler and Walter Ehret

Englewood Cliffs, N. J.: Prentice-Hall, Inc., 1972

Key and Range

1 Arne, Thomas   The lass with the delicate air

2 Bach, J. S.   If thou be near (Bist du bei mir) g,e

3 Beethoven, L. van   The song of the flea (Es war einmal ein König) g,e

4 Böhm, Carl   Calm as the night (Still wie die Nacht) g,e

5 Brahms, Johannes   Sapphic Ode (Sapphische Ode) g,e

6 Caccini, Giulio   Amarilli, my fair one (Amarilli, mia bella) it,e

7 Caldara, Antonio   As from the shining sun (Come raggio di sol) it,e

8 Carpenter, John A.   The sleep that flits on baby's eyes

9 dePue, Wallace   Eldorado

10 dePue, Wallace   Little lamb

11 dePue, Wallace   Lullaby

1

12 Engel, Carl	Sea-shell	
13 Franck, Cesar	O Lord most holy (Panis Angelicus) la,e	
14 Franz, Robert	Dedication (Widmung) g,e	
15 Giordani, G.	Ah, my dear heart (Caro mio ben) it,e	
16 Grieg, Edvard	Boat song	
17 Hahn, Reynaldo	The hour of dreaming (L'heure exquise) fr,e	
18 Handel, G. F.	Beneath these trees (Ombra mai fu) it,e	
19 Handel, G. F.	Where e'er you walk	
20 d'Hardelot, Guy	Because fr,e	
21 Monro, George	My lovely Celia	
22 Purcell, Edward	Passing by	
23 Purcell, Henry	Dido's lament	
24 Quilter, Roger	O mistress mine	
25 Schubert, Franz	Wanderer's night song (Wanderers Nachtlied) g,e	
26 Schubert, Franz	Who is Sylvia, e	
27 So. Mountain Song arr, dePue	He's gone away	

28 Strauss, Richard	The night (Die Nacht) g,e
29 Stravinsky, Igor	Pastorale
30 Sullivan, Arthur	When I was a lad
31 Traditional drinking song	Down among the dead men
32 Vaughan Williams, R.	Silent noon
33 Vaughan Williams, R.	The Vagabond
34 Welsh Folk Song	All through the night
35 Schubert, Franz	Mary, we hail Thee (Ave Maria) la,e
36 Irish Folk Song	Bendemeer's stream

This has been a popular text for many years. I have found much of it to be useful, specifically the illustrations, sections on "General principles of singing," inclusion of blank pages for note-taking and the choice of songs. Unfortunately, at least for use in voice class, I find the ranges too high for some students. There is a list of songs in the back, graded and categorized.

There is no help given the student in how to pronounce the foreign texts.

FOUNDATIONS IN SINGING, 4th Edition

By Van A. Christy

Wm. C. Brown Company, Publishers, 1979

Key and Range

Reg.   Med. High

#	Composer	Title	
37	Appalachian Folk	*Go 'way from my window	
38	Arne, Dr. Thomas	The miller of Mansfield	
39	Beethoven, L. Van	A prayer (Gebet) g,e	
40	Chantey	High barbaree	
41	Christy, Van A.	Peace prayer of St. Francis of Assisi	
42	English Folk Song	Early one morning	
43	English Folk Song	The turtle dove	
44	Franz, Robert	Good night (Gute Nacht) g,e	
45	French Noel	*Sleep of the infant Jesus	
46	Gibbs, C. Armstrong	Five Eyes	
47	Giordani, Giuseppe	Dear love of mine (Caro mio ben) it,e	

4

48 Grieg, Edvard	A swan (Ein Schwan) g,e	
49 Grieg, Edvard	Two brown eyes (Zwei braune Augen) g,e	
50 Haydn, Joseph	Piercing eyes	
51 Homer, Sidney	Requiem	
52 Irish Ballad	The gypsy rover	
53 Irish Folk Song	Bendemeer's stream	
54 Irish Folk Song	Cockles and mussels	
55 Italian Folk Song	Parting (Separazione) it,e	
56 Ives, Charles	At sea	
57 Ives, Charles	At the river	
58 Ives, Charles	Evening	
59 Ives, Charles	The Indians	
60 Ives, Charles	Reminiscence	
61 Jensen, Adolf	O press thy cheek against mine own (Lehn deine Wang' an meine Wang') g,e	
62 Lully, J. B.	Close mine eyes and forever (Fermez vous, pour jamais) fr,e	
63 Mendelssohn, Felix	At parting	

5

64	Monro, George	My lovely Celia	
65	Monteverdi, Claudio	O death, now come (Lasciatemi morire) it,e	
66	Mozart, W. A.	*Great Creator (Ave Verum) lat,e	
67	Nevin, Ethelbert	The rosary	
68	Old French Carol	*March of the three kings	
69	Pergolesi, Giovanni	Nina it,e	
70	Purcell, Henry	Man is for the woman made	
71	Rorem, Ned	A Christmas carol	
72	Rosa, Salvator	Forest, thy green arbors (Selve, voi che le speranze) it,e	
73	Rosa, Salvator	To be near thee (Star vicino) it,e	
74	Rubinstein, Anton	*The angel	
75	Scarlatti, Alessandro	The sun o'er the Ganges (Gia il sole dal Gange) it,e	
76	Schubert, Franz	By the sea (Am Meer) g,e	
77	Schubert, Franz	Morning greeting (Morgengruss) g,e	
78	Schubert, Franz	Night and dreams (Nacht und Träume) g,e	
79	Schubert, Franz	To music (An die Musik) g,e	

6

80 Schubert, Franz — Wanderer's night song (Wanderers Nachtlied) g,e

81 Scottish Ballad — I know where I'm going

82 Spiritual — The Crucifixion ("and He never said a mum'lin word")

83 Spiritual — Walk together chillun

84 Strauss, Richard — *Dear love, I now must leave thee (Ach, Lieb, ich muss nun scheiden) g,e

85 Swedish Folk Song — The dove and the lily

86 Unknown — What if a day

Now in its 4th edition, this well-known text-anthology has added a Medium High to its regular edition, two separate books, identical except for ranges. It is well-organized, contains a considerable amount of information, and includes a 10-page section on foreign language. The songs are well-chosen for variety, including several that can be sung as duets.

* Arranged as solo or optional duet

SONG ANTHOLOGY ONE

Selected, arranged, translated, edited,

and/or composed by Anne and William Leyerle

Leyerle Publications (Box 384, Geneseo, NY), 1977

Key and Range

87 Arne, Dr. Thomas	Arise, sweet messenger of morn	
88 Arne, Dr. Thomas	Blow, blow thou winter wind	
89 Arne, Dr. Thomas	Rule, Britannia	
90 Bach, J. S.	Wert thou with me (Bist du bei mir) g,e	
91 Beach, Mrs. H. H. A.	O mistress mine	
92 Berlioz, Hector	Villanelle fr,e	
93 Brahms, Johannes	Does it often come to mind (Kommt dir manchmal in den Sinn) g,e	
94 Carissimi, Giacomo	Triumphant my heart (Vittoria mio core) it,e	
95 Debussy, Claude	Mandolin (Mandoline) fr,e	
96 Debussy, Claude	Romance, fr,e	
97 Dowland, John	Come again, sweet love	

98	Elgar, Edward	In haven	
99	Elgar, Edward	Where corals lie	
100	Fauré, Gabriel	After a dream (Après un rêve) fr,e	
101	Fisher, W. A.	Sigh no more, ladies	
102	Giordani, Giuseppe	My dearest heart (Caro mio ben) it,e	
103	Handel, G. F.	Ah! my heart (Ah! mio cor) it,e	
104	Handel, G. F.	Never was the shade (Ombra mai fu) it,e	
105	d'Indy, Vincent	Madrigal fr,e	
106	Leyerle, arr.	Black is the color of my true love's hair	
107	Leyerle, arr.	Deep river	
108	Leyerle, arr.	Ev'ry time I feel the spirit	
1 3	Leyerle, arr.	Fare you well	
1 4	Leyerle, arr.	Greensleeves	
111	Leyerle, arr.	Joshua fit the battle of Jericho	
112	Leyerle, arr.	Shenandoah	
113	Leyerle, arr.	Wayfaring stranger	

114 Leoncavallo, R.	A spring rhapsody (Rapsodia Primaverile) it,e	
115 Massenet, Jules	Elegy (Élégie) fr,e	
116 Paisiello, Giovanni	My heart has no more feeling (Nel cor più non mi sento) it,e	
117 Purcell, Henry	Come unto these yellow sands	
118 Purcell, Henry	I attempt from love's sickness to fly	
119 Rosa, Salvator	Changing location is easy (Vado ben spesso) it,e	
120 Schubert, Franz	The organ grinder (Der Leiermann) g,e	
121 Schumann, Robert	Only the longing know (Nur wer die Sehnsucht kennt) g,e	
122 Schumann, Robert	You ring upon my finger (Du Ring an meinem Finger) g,e	
123 Strauss, Richard	Beating hearts (Schlagende Herzen) g,e	
124 Strauss, Richard	Night (Die Nacht) g,e	

This anthology is a song supplement to Wm. Leyerle's Vocal Development through Organic Imagery, and is the first in what they hope will be a series. The songs are well chosen, folk song arrangements are good, and it has the added feature of providing the I P A, commentary on each song, and phonetic transcription with translation of each foreign text. In using this anthology with my beginning voice class, however, I found it somewhat difficult. The ranges (and tessituras) were a little high and those songs with lower ranges were too difficult for the student. Otherwise, a good, solid anthology.

STEPS TO SINGING FOR VOICE CLASSES, 3rd Edition

Royal Stanton

Wadsworth Publishing Company, 1983

Key and Range

Low   High

125 American Folk Song   Down in the valley

126 American Folk Song   He's goin' away

127 American Folk Song   On top of Old Smokey

128 American Folk Song   Poor wayfarin' stranger

129 Appalachian   Black is the color

130 Brahms, Johannes   You fill my heart (Wie bist du, meine Königin) g,e

131 Caldara, Antonio   Tho' not deserving (Sebben, Crudele) it,e

132 Carey, Henry   America

133 Debussy, Claude   When in the setting sun (Beau soir) fr,e

134 Dowland, John   Awake, sweet love

135 Dowland, John   Come again, sweet love

11

136 Folksong	The turtle dove	
137 Franck, Cesar	O Lord most holy (Panis Angelicus) lat,e	
138 Franz, Robert	Dedication (Widmung) g,e	
139 German Folk Song	You, you! (Du, du!) g,e	
140 Gibbons, Orlando	The silver swan	
141 Giordani, Giuseppe	Dear one, believe (Caro mio ben) it,e	
142 Handel, G. F.	Forever blessed	
143 Handel, G. F.	Grant me this favor	
144 Handel, G. F.	Lord, to Thee	
145 Handel, G. F.	Where'er you walk	
146 Handel, G. F.	With thee the desolate moor	
147 Lasso, Orlando di	Take my heart	
148 Mendelssohn, Felix	O rest in the Lord	
149 Old English	Drink to me only with thine eyes	
150 Old English	O dear! what can the matter be	
151 Purcell, Henry	I attempt from love's sickness to fly	

12

152 Rosa, Salvatore	My despair (Star vicino) it,e
153 Schubert, Franz	Litany (Litanei) g,e
154 Schubert, Franz	To music (An die Musik) g,e
155 Scottish	Auld lang syne
156 Spiritual	Go down, Moses
157 Stanton, Royal	Bid me to live
158 Strauss, Richard	Dedication (Zueignung) g,e
159 Sullivan, Arthur	Model of a modern Major-General
160 Traditional	Believe me, if all those endearing young charms
161 Traditional	Old lovesong
162 Traditional	When love is kind
163 Welsh	All through the night

A very good class voice book, the text being thorough but not unnecessarily technical. The song anthology contains 39 songs, sixteen of which are in two keys. The emphasis is on simple songs and short, uncomplicated arrangements. It is the only class voice book that provides songs in two keys in the same volume.

THE VOCAL SOUND

By Barbara Kinsey Sable

Englewood Cliffs, N. J.: Prentice-Hall, Inc., 1982

Key and Range

164 Bach, J. S.   I cling to my love of God (Ich halte
                           treulich still) g,e

165 Beethoven, L. van   I love you dear (Ich liebe dich) g,e

166 Brahms, Johannes   As evening light (In stiller Nacht) g,e

167 Dunhill, Thomas   The cloths of heaven

168 Foster, Stephen   Slumber, my darling

169 Franz, Robert   As the moon's reflection trembles (Wie
                           des Mondes Abbild) g,e

170 Franz, Robert   My love has been awandering (Mein Schatz
                           ist auf der Wanderschaft) g,e

171 Franz, Robert   O wert thou in the cauld blast (O säh ich
                           auf der Heide dort) g,e

172 Fricker, Peter   Vocalise

173 Italian Folk Song   Deep in this soul of mine (Se dentro
                           l'anima) it,e

174 Mozart, W. A.   Emotions of joy (Un moto di gioja) it,e

14

175	Pergolesi, G. B.	If you love me (Se tu m'ami) it,e	
176	Rodgers, R.	Edelweiss	
177	Rodgers, R.	Oh what a beautiful morning	
178	Sable, Barbara	New moon	
179	Scarlatti, A.	The sun is just showing (Gia il sole dal Gange) it,e	
180	Soule, Edmund	The bell-man	
181	Spiritual	Sometimes I feel like a motherless child	
182	Weckerlin, J. B.	Ah, it is pleasant (Ah! qu'il fait beau) fr,e	

Strictly speaking, this volume may not be as useful in class voice as in private teaching. The text is quite detailed and many songs are too difficult. However, it would be an excellent supplement for majors taking private lessons, with chapters on "The Practice Routine," "Health, Fatigue, and Scheduling," "Rules for Performance" and others. Also included are passages for specific voices from vocal literature for practice on long phrases and rapid-note passages. The chapter on "Repertoire" was less satisfying to me.

(See also the review in NATS Bulletin vol. 39, no. 5 (May/ June 1983):38.)

PRINCIPLES OF SINGING

Kenneth E. Miller

Prentice-Hall, Inc., 1983

Key and Range

183 Arne, Michael	The lass with the delicate air	
184 Bach, J. S.	If thou be near (Bist du bei mir) g,e	
185 Bishop, H. R.	Love has eyes	
186 Brahms, J.	Lullaby (Wiegenlied) g,e	
187 Caldara, A.	See the sun's clear rays (Come raggio di sol) it,e	
188 Campion, T.	What if a day	
189 English Folk Song	May-day carol	
190 English Folk Song	The turtle dove	
191 Foster, S.	Jeanie with the light brown hair	
192 Franz, Robert	Dedication (Widmung) g,e	
193 Giordani, G.	Ah, dearest love (Caro mio ben) it,e	

194 Godard, B.   Florian's song (Chanson de Florian) fr,e

195 Grieg, E.   I love thee (Ich liebe dich) g,e

196 Grieg, E.   A swan (Ein Schwan) g,e

197 Handel, G. F.   Where'er you walk

198 Ives, Charles   When stars are in the quiet skies

199 Jensen, A.   Oh press thy cheek against mine own
                        (Lehn' deine Wang' an meine Wang') g,e

200 Mendelssohn, F.   Folk song (Volkslied) g,e

201 Mendelssohn, F.   O rest in the Lord

202 Monroe, G.   My lovely Celia

203 Morley, T.   It was a lover and his lass

204 Negro spiritual   Sometimes I feel like a motherless child

205 Paisiello, G.   My heart ne'er leaps with gladness
                        (Nel cor piu non mi sento) it,e

206 Pergolesi, G. B.   Nina it,e

207 Purcell, E.   Passing by

208 Purcell, H.   Man is for the woman made

209 Rorem, Ned   A Christmas carol

210	Rosa, S.	To be near thee (Star vicino) it,e
211	Scarlatti, A.	O relent, no more torment me (O cessate di piagarmi) it,e
212	Scarlatti, A.	O'er the Ganges now rises (Gia il sole dal Gange) it,e
213	Schubert, F.	Ave Maria la,e
214	Schubert, F.	The little rosebud (Heidenröslein) g,e
215	Schubert, F.	Serenade (Ständchen) g,e
216	Schubert, F.	To music (An die musik) g,e
217	Schubert, F.	Who is Sylvia (An Sylvia) g,e
218	Vaughan Williams, R.	Greensleeves
219	Welsh air	All through the night

This is a new entry in the area of class voice, and, it seems to me, one of the better ones. Explanations are clear, accurate and concise and the 37 songs represent a variety of styles and languages. In addition to the usual material, there are excellent chapters on English and foreign language pronunciation, and vocalises in three ranges taken from Sieber, Concone and Vaccai.

B. Bibliography

Abusamra, Ward. "Small Group vs Individual Instruction in the Performance Studio," <u>NATS</u> <u>Bulletin</u> 34, no. 4 (May, 1978): 37-38.

Antahades, Mary Ella. "Singing Reaches Out: Creative Use of Class Voice and 'Packaging,'" <u>NATS</u> <u>Bulletin</u> 30, no. 2 (December, 1973): 12-17, 31, 39.

Bang, B. "Small Flute Classes: Less Teaching, More Learning," <u>Music</u> <u>Educators</u> <u>Journal</u> 57 (October, 1970): 49-51.

Barresi, A. L. and H. Simons. "Voice Classes Won't Work in My School! (Really?)," <u>Music</u> <u>Educators</u> <u>Journal</u> 56 (September, 1969): 80.

Brand, M. "Toward Greater Teaching Effectiveness," <u>College</u> <u>Music</u> <u>Symposium</u>, 20, no. 2 (1980): 138-41.

Brun, A. J. "Advantages of Class Instruction," <u>Music</u> <u>Journal</u>, 30 (October 1972): 28-29.

Christy, Van. "Class Voice: Its Character, Method, Values, Advantages, Weaknesses, Activities, and Objectives," in <u>Expressive</u> <u>Singing</u>, volume two. Dubuque, Iowa: Wm C. Brown Co., 1975.

Corder, D. L. "Intermediate and Advanced Level Group Instruction in Under-graduate Applied Music: A Survey and Analysis," <u>Dissertation</u> <u>Abstracts</u>, 39 (January 1979): 4108A.

Doscher, Barbara. "The Beginning Voice Class," <u>NATS</u> <u>Bulletin</u>, 32, no. 1 (October 1975): 33-35.

Duckworth, Guy and R. Dean Lund. "Reducing Teacher Time in Multi-Student Settings for Performance Instruction," <u>College</u> <u>Music</u> <u>Symposium</u>, 15 (Spring 1975): 100-108.

-------. "Innovative Programs in Performance Studies: Group and Class Instruction," <u>College</u> <u>Music</u> <u>Symposium</u>, 13 (Fall 1973).

Hardy, D. "Group Teaching - A Complete Preparation," <u>American</u> <u>Music</u> <u>Teacher</u>, 30, no. 1 (1980): 18-19.

Hill, J. R. "An Instructional Program for High School Vocal Music Performance Classes Based Upon Recent Theories of Aesthetic Perception and Response," <u>Dissertation</u> <u>Abstracts</u>, 41 (March 1981): 3936A.

Johnson, Sarah O. "Group Instruction: An Alternative for Freshman Voice Students," <u>NATS</u> <u>Bulletin</u>, 35, no. 4 (March/April 1979): 20-21.

Jones, L. "The Future of Applied Voice in Colleges and Universities," NATS Bulletin, 22, no. 4 (May 1966): 30-32.

Kinsey, Barbara. "Voice Class: Structure and Purpose," NATS Bulletin, 30, no. 2 (December 1973): 18-22.

Lewis, Pamela Payne. "The Class Voice Journal: Using Writing to Improve Singing," NATS Bulletin, 38, no. 2 (November/December 1981): 33-36.

Pearce, E. T. "Group Lessons: A Plus for the Private Student," American Music Teacher, 27, no. 6 (1978): 22-23.

Rogers, G. L. "Private vs Class Instruction," The Instrumentalist, 34 (February 1980): 106.

Rolland, P. "Class Teaching? . . . ? Private Teaching?" The School Musician, 30 (March 1959): 40-41.

Schneider, Dorothy. "Procedures in the Voice Class," NATS Bulletin, 15, no. 3 (February 15, 1959): 4-5. Reprinted in NATS Bulletin, 29, no. 3 (Feb/March 1973): 42.

Seipp, N. F. "A Comparison of Class and Private Music Instruction," Dissertation Abstracts, 37 (June 1977):7602A-7603A.

Silverman, R. "Private vs Class Instruction, the Heteroeneous Instrumental Class," The Instrumentalist, 36 (November 1981): 130.

Sims, F. J. "An Experimental Investigation of the Relative Effectiveness of Group and Individual Voice Instruction at the Beginning Level to High School Students," Dissertation Abstracts, 22 (November 1961):1659.

Tipton, A. "Is There a Stigma To Class Teaching of a Solo Instrument?" The School Musician, 44 (May 1973): 22-23.

Vogel, D. E. "An Empirical Look at Combined Group and Private Voice Studio Teaching," NATS Bulletin, 33, no. 2 (Dec. 1976):20-21.

Woolridge, Warren, "Why not Class Voice?" NATS Bulletin 28, no. 2 (Dec. 1971): 20-21.

PATHWAYS OF SONG, Vol. I

Edited by LaForge and Earhart

Published by M. Witmark and Sons, 1934

Key and Range

		Low	High

220 Colasse, Pascal — To thy fair charm (Tout cede a vos doux appas) fr,e

221 Czech Folk Song — Dance song

222 Czech Folk Song — The falling dew

223 Czech Folk Song — Maiden tell me

224 Czech Folk Song — Secret love

225 Franck, Cesar — Heavenly manna (Panis Angelicus) lat,e

226 Franz, Robert — A Woodland journey (Waldfahrt) g,e

227 Franz, Robert — Feast of love (Liebesfeier) g,e

228 Franz, Robert — For music (Für Musik) g,e

229 German Folk Song — The Sandman

230 Grieg, Edvard — The First primrose (Mit einer Primula veris) g,e

21

231 Handel, G. F.   Grace thy fair brow (Rend'il sereno al ciglio) it,e

232 Handel, G. F.   Verdant meadows (Verdi Prati) it,e

233 Haydn, F. J.   In the country (Die Landlust) g,e

234 Liszt, Franz   It must be wonderful indeed (Es muss ein Wunderbares sein) g,e

235 Mozart, W. A.   Cradle song (Wiegenlied) g,e

236 Mozart, W. A.   Longing for spring

237 Purcell, Edward   Passing by

238 Schubert, Franz   Farewell (Adieu!) fr,e

239 Schubert, Franz   In evening's glow (Im Abendrot) g,e

240 Schumann, Robert   The lotus flower (Die Lotosblume) g,e

241 Schumann, Robert   Snowbells (Schneeglöckchen) g,e

242 Schumann, Robert   To the sunshine (An den Sonnenschein) g,e

(For comment see page 28)

PATHWAYS OF SONG, Vol. II

Edited by LaForge and Earhart

Published by M. Witmark and Sons, 1934

Key and Range

Low   High

243 Bach, J. S.   If thou be near (Bist du bei mir) g,e

244 Bayly, T. H.   Oh, 'tis the melody

245 Beethoven, L. van   I love thee (Ich liebe dich) g,e

246 Beethoven, L. van   To the beloved (An die Geliebte) g,e

247 Brahms, Johannes   Below in the valley (Da unten im Tale) g,e

248 Brahms, Johannes   Cradle song (Wiegenlied) g,e

249 Brahms, Johannes   My dear one's mouth is like the rose (Mein Mädel hat einen Rosenmund) g,e

250 Fauré, Gabriel   The cradles (Les Berceaux) fr,e

251 Franck, Cesar   Lied, fr,e

252 Franz, Robert   Dedication (Widmung) g,e

253 Franz, Robert   Farewell (Gute Nacht) g,e

23

254 Franz, Robert	Request (Bitte) g,e	
255 German Folk-song	The mill-wheel (Das Mühlrad) g,e	
256 Handel, G. F.	Leave me in sorrow (Lascia ch'io pianga) it,e	
257 Handel, G. F.	Ne'er shade so dear (Ombra mai fu) it, e	
258 Haydn, Joseph	Serenade (Liebes Mädchen, hör' mir zu) g,e	
259 Haydn, Joseph	To friendship (An die Freundschaft) g,e	
260 Hefferman, I.	Watchman's song	
261 Irish air, arr. Earhart	Eileen Aroon	
262 Lully, J. B.	By the light of the moon (Au clair de la lune) fr,e	
263 Old Provencal	March of the kings (La march des rois) fr,e	
264 Old Provencal	The song of the drummer (La chanson du tambourineur) fr,e	
265 Schubert, Franz	Calm at sea (Meeresstilee) g,e	

PATHWAYS OF SONG, Vol. III

Edited by LaForge and Earhart

Published by M. Witmark and Sons, 1934

Key and Range

Low   High

266 Anonymous   Have you seen but a whyte lillie
                           grow

267 Anonymous   When love is kind

268 Bach, J. S.   Come, sweet death (Komm, süsser
                           Tod) g,e

269 Beethoven, L. van   The kiss (Der Kuss) g,e

270 Bishop, Henry   Love has eyes

271 Bohemian Folksong   Plaint (Stesk) b,e

272 Caccini, Giulio   Amarilli, it,e

273 Debussy   There's weeping in my heart (Il
                           pleure dans mon coeur) fr,e

274 Durante, Francesco   Dance, maiden, dance (Danza,
                           danza fanciulla) it,e

275 Franz, Robert   Hark! How still (Stille sicherheit)
                           g,e

276 Franz, Robert   The rose complains (Es hat die
                           Rose sich beklagt) g,e

277 Giovannini (att. to Bach)	Wilt thou thy heart surrender (Willst du dein Herz mir schenken) g,e	
278 Gluck, C. W. von	Beloved strand (Spiagge amate) it,e	
279 Grieg, Edvard	The first meeting (Erstes Begegnen) g,e	
280 Grieg, Edvard	With a water-lily (Mit einer Wasser-lillie) g,e	
281 Handel, G. F.	Air (Care selve) it,e	
282 Handel, G. F.	Oh, sleep! why dost thou leave me?	
283 Irish Folk-song	Kitty of Coleraine	
284 Leveridge, Richard	Love is a bauble	
285 Rosa, Salvator	To be near thee (Star vicino) it,e	
286 Scarlatti, A.	The sun o'er the Ganges (Gia il sole dal Gange) it,e	
287 Schubert, Franz	Cradle song (Wiegenlied) g,e	
288 Spanish Folk-song	I don't wish to marry (No quiero casarme) sp,e	
289 Torelli, Giuseppe	Thou knowest well (Tu lo sai) it,e	

PATHWAYS OF SONG, Vol. IV

Edited by LaForge and Earhart

Published by M. Witmark and Sons, 1934

Key and Range

Low   High

290 Bach, J. S.   Blessed Redeemer (Liebster Herr
                           Jesu) g,e

291 Bach, J. S.   Golden sun streaming (Die gold'ne
                           Sonne, voll Freud' und Wonne) g,e

292 Bohemian Folk Song   Sleep, little angel

293 Caldara, Antonio   As from the sun a ray (Come raggio
                           di sol) it,e

294 Caldara, Antonio   Soul of my heart (Alma del core)
                           it,e

295 Debussy, Claude   The Bells (Les cloches) fr,e

296 German Folk Song   Now suffer me, fair maiden
                           (Erlaube mir, fein's Mädchen) g,e

297 German Folk Song   To part, ah, grief unending (Ach,
                           Gott, wie weh tat Scheiden) g,e

298 Grieg, Edvard   Good morning (God Morgen) g,e

299 Grieg, Edvard   Mother

300 Grieg, Edvard   Return to the mountain home (Auf
                           der Reise zur Heimat) g,e

27

301 Handel, G. F.	Here amid the shady woods		
302 Handel, G. F.	Vouchsafe, O Lord		
303 Haydn, F. J.	A very ordinary story (Eine sehr gewöhnliche Geschichte) g,e		
304 Haydn, F. J.	Equals (Der Gleichsinn) g,e		
305 Neapolitan Folk Song	Cicerenella, it,e		
306 Russian Folk Song	Ah, no stormy wind		
307 Russian Folk Song	The jailer's slumber song		
308 Schubert, Franz	Heaven-rays (Himmelsfunken) g,e		
309 Schubert, Franz	Night and dreams (Nacht und Träume) g,e		
310 Schubert, Franz	Now love has falsely played me (Die Liebe hat gelogen) g,e		
311 Schumann, Robert	The rose and the lily (Die Rose, die Lilie, die Taube) g,e		
312 Schumann, Robert	The song of the nightingale (Wehmut) g,e		
313 Schumann, Robert	Thou art a tender blossom (Du bist wie eine Blume) g,e		
314 Strauss, Richard	Night (Die Nacht) g,e		
315 Strauss, Richard	Tomorrow (Morgen) g,e		

Taken together, these four volumes present an excellent
selection of songs. Separately, they are not as useable.

SEVEN CENTURIES OF SOLO SONG, Vol. I

Edited by James Woodside

Published by Boston Music Co., 1943

Key and Range

Low   High

316 Albert, Heinrich — Bless'd is he (O wie gross ist doch der Mann) g,e

317 Anonymous — Have you seen but a whyte lillie grow

318 Arne, Thomas A. — Blow, blow thou winter wind

319 Bach, J. S. — Stay thou near by (Bist du bei mir) g,e

320 Beethoven, L. van — In this dark tomb (In questa tomba) it,e

321 Beethoven, L. van — The kiss (Der Kuss) g,e

322 Caccini, Giulio — Immortal eyes (Occhi immortale) it,e

323 Campion, Thomas — Never weather-beaten sail

324 Dowland, John — Awake, sweet love

325 Giordani, Giuseppe — Light of my day (Caro mio ben) it,e

326 Gluck, C. W. — Thou art, my dear beloved (O del mio dolce ardor) it,e

29

327 de la Halle, Adam   With amorous heart (D'amorous cuer) fr,e

328 Handel, G. F.   Come and trip it

329 Haydn, Joseph   A very commonplace story (Ein sehr gewöhnliche Geschichte) g,e

330 Hopkinson, Francis   My days have been so wondrous free

331 Lawes, Henry   The nightingale

332 Lully, Jean-Baptiste   Gloomy woods (Bois épais) fr,e

333 deMachault, Guillaume   The gallant (C'est force faire le weil) fr,e

334 Martini, Jean Paul   The joys of love (Plaisir d'amour) fr,e

335 Milan, Luis   Ah! Could I but conquer love (Al amor quierro vencer) sp,e

336 Monteverdi, Claudio   O death, pray come (Lasciatemi morire) it,e

337 Monteverdi, Claudio   So sweet is the torment (Si dolce e'l tormento) it,e

338 Morley, Thomas   It was a lover and his lasse

339 Mozart, W. A.   Gay laughter awakens (Ridente la calma) it,e

340 Purcell, Henry   The knotting song

341 Rameau, Jean Philippe   The musette (La musette) fr,e

342 Scarlatti, Alessandro   Fortune (La fortuna) it,e

343 Schubert, Franz   The town (Die Stadt) g,e

344 Storace, Stephen   The pretty creature

345 von Wolkenstein, Oswald   O beautiful month of May
                                        (Im mai) g,e

SEVEN CENTURIES OF SOLO SONG, Vol. II

Edited by James Woodside

Published by Boston Music Company, 1943

Key and Range

Low   High

346 American Folk-song, arr.   Bird courtships
      Woodside

347 Borodin, Alexander   Arabian melody

348 Brahms, Johannes   Serenade (Ständchen) g,e

349 Debussy, Claude   Beautiful evening (Beau soir)
                                   fr,e

350 Duparc, Henri   Lament (Lamento) fr,e

351 English Folk-song, arr.   The miller of Dee
      Beethoven

352 Fauré, Gabriel   Song of the harvesters (La
                                   ronde des moissonneurs) fr,e

353 Franck, Cesar   O Lord most holy (Panis Angelicus)
                                   l,e

354 Franz, Robert   Stars with tiny feet (Sterne mit
                                   den gold'nen Füsschen) g,e

355 French Brunette, arr.   O nightingale (Du rossignol qui
      Weckerlin   chante) fr,e

356 French Colonial, arr.   Lizette
      Weckerlin

357 German Folk-song, arr. Brahms — Yon maiden's lips are rosy red (Mein Mädel hat einen Rosenmund) g,e

358 Gretchaninoff, Alex. — Land of mine

359 Grieg, Edvard — Why with tears softly shimm'ring? (Hvorfor svømmer dit øge) n,e

360 Griffes, Charles — We'll to the woods and gather May

361 Hungarian Folk-song, arr. Woodside — Autumn

362 Irish Folk-song, arr. Beethoven — Dermot and Shelah

363 MacDowell, Edward — The blue-bell

364 MacDowell, Edward — The myrtle

365 Moussorgsky, Modest — Tiny star, where art thou?

366 Norwegian Folk-song, arr. Woodside — To fold, ye lambkins

367 Paladilhe, Emile — I said to the starlets (J'ai dit aux étoiles) fr,e

368 Pyrenean Folk-song, arr. Middlemore — I like them all (Me gustan todas) sp,e

369 Respighi, Ottorino — Mists (Nebbie) it,e

370 Rimsky-Korsakoff, N. — The nightingale

371 Russian Folk-song, arr. Woodside — Cossack cradle song

372 Schumann, Robert — Wildwood rose (Röselein, Röselein) g,e

33

373 Scottish Folk-song, arr.   I lo'e ne'er a laddie but ane
    Haydn

374 Strauss, Richard   Dedication (Zueignung) g,e

375 Treharne, Bryceson   A widow bird sat mourning

376 Venetian Folk-song, arr.   The gondola (La gondoletta) it,e
    Beethoven

377 Welsh Folk-song, arr.   The blossom of the thorn
    Haydn

378 Wolf, Hugo   Prayer (Gebet) g,e

The original six volumes of this excellent series have been
condensed into two, making it much more practical and easy
to use. There is good selection of songs, ranges are
never excessive, and at $8.00 per volume (at this writing)
is a very good value.

THE YOUNG SINGER, SOPRANO

Book One

Edited by Richard B. Row

Row Music Company Inc., Carl Fischer Inc., distributors, 1965

Key and Range

379	American Folk Song	Jesus, Jesus rest your head	
380	Beach, BHA	The year's at the spring	
381	Bishop, Henry	Love has eyes	
382	Carey, Henry	A pastoral	
383	Delibes, Leo	Good morning, Sue! (bonjour, Suzon) fr,e	
384	Dvorak, Anton	Songs my mother taught me (Als die alte Mutter) g,e	
385	Foote, Arthur	I'm wearing awa' to the land o' the leal	
386	Franz, Robert	Dedication (Widmung) g,e	
387	Franz, Robert	For music (Für Musik) g,e	
388	Franz, Robert	Pleading (Bitte) g,e	
389	German, Edward	Who'll buy my lavender	

390	Grieg, Edvard	A Swan (Ein Schwan) g,e	
391	Grieg, Edvard	I love thee (Ich liebe dich) g,e	
392	Handel, G. F.	Care selve, it	
393	Hawley, C. B.	The sweetest flower that blows	
394	Haydn, Joseph	My mother bids me bind my hair (Bind' auf dein Haar) g,e	
395	Horn, E. Charles	I've been roaming	
396	Lehmann, Liza	The cuckoo	
397	Lohr, Hermann	The little Irish girl	
398	MacDowell, Edward	Thy beaming eyes	
399	Mendelssohn, Felix	On wings of song (Auf Flügeln des Gesanges) g,e	
400	Old English	When love is kind	
401	Purcell, Edward	Passing by	
402	Purcell, Henry	Nymphs and shepherds	
403	Sinding, Christian	Sylvelin, g,e	
404	Strauss, Richard	Tomorrow (Morgen) g,e	
405	Swedish Folksong	When I was seventeen	

THE YOUNG SINGER, CONTRALTO (MEZZO-SOPRANO)

Book One

Edited by Richard D. Row

Row Music Company Inc., Carl Fischer Inc., Distributors, 1965

Key and Range

406	American Folk Song	Jesus, Jesus, rest your head
407	Bishop, Henry	Love has eyes
408	Brahms, Johannes	Sapphic Ode (Sapphische Ode) g,e
409	Carey, Henry	A pastoral
410	Dvorak, Anton	Songs my mother taught me (Als die alte Mutter) g,e
411	Foote, Arthur	I'm wearing awa' to the land o' the leal
412	Franz, Robert	For music (Für Musik) g,e
413	Franz, Robert	Pleading (Bitte) g,e
414	German, Edward	Who'll buy my lavender
415	Grieg, Edvard	A swan (Ein Schwan) g,e
416	Haydn, Josef	She never told her love

417	Henschel, Georg	Morning hymn (Morgen-Hymne) g,e
418	Lehmann, Liza	The cuckoo
419	Lohr, Hermann	The little Irish girl
420	MacDowell, Edward	Thy beaming eyes
421	Mendelssohn, Felix	On wings of song (Auf Flügeln des Gesanges) g,e
422	Old English	When love is kind
423	Purcell, Edward	Passing by
424	Purcell, Henry	Nymphs and shepherds
425	Quilter, Roger	Now sleeps the crimson petal
426	Reichardt, Louise	When roses bloom (Hoffnung) g,e
427	Respighi, Ottorino	Mists (Nebbie) it,e
428	Scott, Lady John	Think on me
429	Sinding, Christian	Sylvelin, g,e
430	Strauss, Richard	Tomorrow (Morgen) g,e

THE YOUNG SINGER, TENOR

Book One

Edited by Richard D. Row

Row Music Company Inc., Carl Fischer Inc., Distributors, 1965

Key and Range

431 American Folk Song   Jesus, Jesus, rest your head

432 Bartlett, J. C.   A dream

433 Bishop, Sir Henry   Love has eyes

434 Dix, J. Airlie   The Trumpeter

435 Foote, Arthur   I'm wearing awa' to the land o' the leal

436 Franz, Robert   For music (Für Musik) g,e

437 Franz, Robert   Pleading (Bitte) g,e

438 German, Edward   Rolling down to Rio

439 Grieg, Edvard   A swan (Ein Schwan) g,e

440 Grieg, Edvard   I love thee (Ich liebe dich) g,e

441 Handel, G. F.   Care selve, it

442	Handel, G. F.	Where'er you walk
443	Haydn, Joseph	Serenade (Liebes Mädchen) g,e
444	Homer, Sidney	Requiem
445	Lohr, Hermann	The little Irish Girl
446	MacDowell, Edward	Thy beaming eyes
447	Mendelssohn, Felix	On wings of song (Auf Flügeln des Gesanges) g,e
448	Metcalf, John W.	The night has a thousand eyes
449	Monro, Georg	My lovely Celia
450	Purcell, Edward	Passing by
451	Quilter, Roger	Now sleeps the crimson petal
452	Rachmaninoff, S.	How fair this spot (Tout est si beau) fr,e
453	Respighi, Ottorino	Mists (Nebbie) it,e
454	Sinding, Christian	Sylvelin, g,e
455	Strauss, Richard	Tomorrow (Morgen) g,e
456	Tchaikovsky, Peter	Pilgrim's song

THE YOUNG SINGER, BARITONE

Book One

Compiled and Edited by Richard D. Row

Row Music Company Inc., Carl Fischer Inc., Distributors, 1965

Key and Range

457 American Folk Song,   Jesus, Jesus, rest your head
    arr. Row

458 Bishop, Henry   Love has eyes

459 Dix, J. Airlie   The Trumpeter

460 Foote, Arthur   I'm wearing awa' to the land o' the leal

461 Franz, Robert   Dedication (Widmung) g,e

462 Franz, Robert   For Music (Für Musik) g,e

463 German, Edward   Rolling down to Rio

464 Grieg, Edvard   A Swan (Ein Schwan) g,e

465 Handel, G. F.   When first we met (Ptolemy)

466 Handel, G. F.   Where'er you walk (Semele)

467 Haydn, Joseph   Serenade (Liebes Mädchen, hör'mir zu) g,e

41

468	Homer, Signey	Requiem
469	Lühr, Herman	The little Irish girl
470	Mendelssohn, Felix	On wings of song (Auf Flügeln des Gesanges) g,e
471	Old English	Come let's be merry
472	Purcell, Edward	Passing by
473	Quilter, Roger	Now sleeps the crimson petal
474	Reichardt, Louise	When the roses bloom (Hoffnung) g,e
475	Respighi, Ottorino	Mists (Nebbie)
476	Strauss, Richard	Tomorrow (Morgen) g,e
477	Tschaikowsky, Peter	Pilgrim's song
478	Vaughan Williams, R.	The roadside fire
479	Vaughan Williams, R.	Silent noon

I am fond of these four anthologies and have used them often with my younger or inexperienced students. There is much that can be taught from them in early developmental stages.

42

EXPRESSIVE SINGING SONG ANTHOLOGY VOLUME ONE

Edited by Van A. Christy

Wm. C. Brown Company, Publishers

First Edition 1966, Second Edition 1983

		Low	Medium	High
480 Adam, Stephen	The holy city			
481 Beethoven, L. van	I love thee (Ich liebe dich) g,e			
482 Beethoven, L. van	The miller of Dee			
483 Böhm, Carl	Still as the night (Still wie die Nacht) g,e			
484 Brahms, Johannes	Far down in the valley (Da unten im Tale) g,e			
485 Christy, Van (arr)	All through the night (Welsh)			
486 Christy, Van (arr)	Away over Yandro (Southern Mountain)			
487 Christy, Van (arr)	Beautiful Savior (Crusaders' Hymn)			
488 Christy, Van (arr)	Begone dull care (Old English) (Duet)			
489 Christy, Van (arr)	Joshua fit the battle of Jericho			
490 Christy, Van (arr)	Lonesome valley (white spiritual)			

43

491 Christy, Van (arr)	Mister banjo (Creole)	
492 Christy, Van (arr)	O calm of night (Suabian) (Duet)	
493 Christy, Van (arr)	Shenandoah (Chantey)	
494 Christy, Van (arr)	Tutu Maramba (Brazilian Lullaby)	
495 Christy, Van (arr)	The old woman and the peddler (English)	
496 Chopin, Frederic	Lithuanian song (Lithauisches Lied) g,e	
497 Dvorak, Anton	Songs my mother taught me (Als die alte Mutter) g,e	
498 Fontenailles, H de	A resolve (Obstination) fr,e	
499 Franck, Cesar	Bread of angels (Panis Angelicus) l,e (Duet)	
500 Franz, Robert	Dedication (Widmung) g,e	
501 Franz, Robert	Out of my soul's great sadness (Aus meinen grossen Schmerzen) g,e	
502 Gaul, Alfred	Eye hath not seen (from "The Holy City")	
503 Grieg, Edvard	I love thee (Ich liebe dich) g,e	
504 Handel, G. F.	Verdant Meadows (Verdi prati) it,e (Duet)	
505 Handel, G. F.	Where'er you walk (from "Semele")	
506 Haydn, Joseph	A very commonplace story (Ein sehr ge- wöhnliche Geschichte) g,e	

44

507 Haydn, Joseph	She never told her love	
508 Lully, J. B.	Sombre woods (Bois épais) fr,e	
509 MacDowell, Edward	The sea	
510 Martini, Giovanni	The joys of love (plaisir d'amour) fr,e	
511 Mellish, Col. R.	Drink to me only with thine eyes (Old English Air)	
512 Mendelssohn, Felix	On wings of music (Auf Flügeln des Gesanges) g,e (Duet)	
513 Mendelssohn, Felix	O rest in the Lord (from "Elijah")	
514 Mozart, W. A.	A tragic story	
515 Nevin, Ethelbert	Little boy blue	
516 Purcell, Edward	Passing by	
517 Schubert, Franz	Faith in spring (Frühlingsglaube) g,e	
518 Schumann, Robert	The lotus flower (Die Lotosblume) g,e	
519 Schumann, Robert	Thou'rt lovely as a flower (Du bist wie eine Blume) g,e	
520 Scott, Lady	Think on me	
521 Sullivan, Arthur	The lost chord	
522 Tchaikovsky, Peter	A legend	

523 Tchaikovsky, Peter — None but the lonely heart (Nur wer die Sehn-sucht kennt) g,e

524 Wilson, H. Lane — The pretty creature (Old English)

The second edition of Vol. I has 55 songs and sells for about $20. Of the eleven songs new to this edition, six appear in Mr. Christy's <u>Foundations in Singing</u> and are marked here with an asterisk.

525 Caccini, G. — Amarilli it,e

526 Caldara, A. — Tho' not deserving (Sebben, crudele) it,e

527*Christy, Van — Go 'way from my window

528 Christy, Van — Poor wayfaring stranger

529*Franz, Robert — Good night (Gute Nacht) g,e

530*Grieg, Edvard — Two brown eyes (Zwei braune Auge) g,e

531*Homer, Sidney — Requiem

532*Mozart — Great Creator (Ave verum) la,e

533 Paisiello, G. — Why feels my heart so dormant (Nel cor piu non mi sento) it,e

534 Scarlatti, A. — Oh no longer seek to pain me (O cessate di piagarmi) it,e

535*Schubert, F. — Morning greeting (Morgengruss) g,e

EXPRESSIVE SINGING SONG ANTHOLOGY

VOLUME TWO

Edited by Van A. Christy

Wm. C. Brown Co., Publishers, 1966

		Low	Medium	High
536 Arne, Thomas A.	The lass with the delicate air			
537 Beethoven, L. van	To the distant beloved (An die ferne Geliebte) g,e			
538 Bishop, Sir Henry	Love has eyes			
539 Brahms, Johannes	Sapphic ode (Sapphische Ode) g,e			
540 Caldara, Antonio	When on the surging wave (Come raggio di sol) it,e			
541 Carey, Henry	A pastoral			
542 Debussy, Claude	Evening fair (Beau soir) fr,e			
543 Durante, Francesco	Virgin, fount of love (Vergin, tutto amor) it,e			
544 Fauré, Gabriel	After a dream (Apres un rêve) fr,e			
545 Fauré, Gabriel	The cradles (Les Berceaux) fr,e			
546 Giordani, Giuseppe	Dear love of mine (Caro mio ben) it,e			

47

547 Godard, Benjamin	Florian's song (Chanson de Florian) fr,e	
548 Gounod, Charles	O, divine redeemer (Repentir) fr,e (Duet)	
549 Hahn, Reynaldo	The exquisite hour (L'heure exquise) fr,e	
550 Hahn, Reynaldo	Were my songs with wings provided (Si mes vers avaient des ailes) fr,e	
551 Handel, G. F.	Ah, poor heart (Ah, mio cor, from "Alcina")it,e	
552 Handel, G. F.	Leave me to languish (Lascia ch'io pianga) it,e	
553 Handel, G. F.	Oh, sleep, why dost thou leave me (from "Semele")	
554 Handel, G. F.	O lovely peace (from "Judas Maccabaeus") Duet	
555 Handel, G. F.	Weep no more (from "Hercules")	
556 Hue, Georges	I wept, beloved, as I dreamed (J'ai pleuré en reve) fr,e	
557 Lalo, Edouard	The captive (L'esclave) fr,e	
558 Legrenzi, Giovanni	With cunning conniving (Che fiero costume) it,e	
559 Lotti, Antonio	Speak once more, dear (Pur dicesti, o bocca bella) it,e	
560 Massenet, Jules	Elegy (Élégie) fr,e	
561 Monro, George	My lovely Celia	
562 Monteverdi, Claudio	O death now come (Lasciatemi morire) it,e	

48

563 Pergolesi, G. B.   Nina it,e

564 Purcell, Henry   Come unto these yellow sands (Duet)

565 Purcell, Henry   Dido's lament (from "Dido and Aeneas")

566 Purcell, Henry   I attempt from love's sickness

567 Purcell, Henry   Sound the trumpet (Duet)

568 Rosa, Salvator   To be near thee (Star vicino) it,e

569 Schubert, Franz   Impatience (Ungeduld) g,e

570 Schubert, Franz   Serenade (Ständchen) g,e (Duet)

571 Schumann, Robert   I dreamed that I was weeping (Ich hab' im traum geweinet) g,e

572 Schumann, Robert   I'll not complain (Ich grolle nicht) g,e

573 Stradella, Alessandro   O Lord, have mercy (Pieta, Signore) it,e

574 Strauss, Richard   All Soul's day (Aller-seelen) g,e

575 Strauss, Richard   Tomorrow (Morgen) g,e

576 Strauss, Richard   To you (Zueignung) g,e

577 Sullivan, Arthur   Orpheus with his lute

578 Torelli, Giuseppe   Well thou knowest (Tu lo sai) it,e

579 Wolf, Hugo   Secrecy (Verborgenheit)
                        g,e

At this writing, still in 1st edition. A good
collection and the idea of having three keys
available is excellent. However, it is getting
more and more expensive. One must carefully
weigh the cost against expected use.

STANDARD VOCAL REPERTOIRE, Book One

Collected, edited and arranged by R. D. Row

R. D. Row Music Co., Inc., 1959

Key and Range

Low   High

580 Arne, Dr. Thomas   Air (from "Comus")

581 Bennett, Charles   The guitar player

582 D'Hardelot, Guy   Because fr,e

583 Folk-song   Fare you well   *NOT IN HIGH VOICE*

584 Folk-song   Cockles and mussels

585 Franz, Robert   Dedication (Widmung) g,e

586 Grieg, Edvard   I love thee (Ich liebe dich) g,e

587 Handel, G. F.   When first we met (from "Ptolemy")

588 Handel, G. F.   Where'er you walk (from "Semele")

589 Handel, G. F.   Would you gain the tender creature (from "Acis and Galatea")   *NOT IN LOW VOICE*

590 Haydn, F. J.   My mother bids me bind my hair (Bind' auf dein Haar) g,e   *NOT IN LOW VOICE*

51

591	Haydn, F. J.	Sailor's song	
592	Haydn, F. J.	She never told her love	
593	Haydn, F. J.	The wanderer (Der Wanderer) g,e	
594	Lehmann, Liza	The cuckoo	
595	Linley, Thomas	No flower that blows	
596	Monro, George	My lovely Celia	
597	Mozart, W. A.	Ridente la calma it	
598	Purcell, Edward	Passing by	
599	Purcell, Henry	Hush, be silent	
600	Purcell, Henry	If music be the food of love	
601	Purcell, Henry	Strike the viol	
602	Purcell, Henry	The arrival of the royal barge	
603	Rachmaninoff, S.	In the silent night	
604	Reichardt, Louise	When the roses bloom (Hoffnung) g,e	
605	Schubert, Franz	The shepherdess (La Pastorella) it,e	
606	Scott, Lady John	Think on me	

52

STANDARD VOCAL REPERTOIRE, Book Two

Edited by R. D. Row

R. D. Row Music Company, Inc., 1963

Key and Range

Low   High

607 Bemberg, H.   'Tis snowing (Il neige) fr,e

608 Bennett, Charles   Japanese night song

609 Boardman, Reginald   Cindy

610 Chopin, Frederic   The maiden's wish (Mädchen's
                             Wunsch) g,e

611 Debussy, Claude   Night of starlight (Nuit
                             d'ètoiles) fr,e

612 Franz, Robert   Mother, o sing me to rest
                             (Mutter, o sing mich zur Ruh')
                             g,e

613 Handel, G. F.   Care selve it

614 Handel, G. F.   Friendship and song

615 Handel, G. F.   Peace unto you from heaven
                             (Rend'il sereno al ciglio) it,e

616 Hawley, C. B.   The sweetest flower that blows

617 Haydn, F. J.   Serenade g,e

618	Henschel, Georg	Morning Hymn (Morgen-Hymne) g,e
619	Löhr, Herman	The little Irish girl
620	Lully, J. B.	Sombre woods (Bois épais) fr,e
621	Metcalf, John W.	The night has a thousand eyes
622	Mozart, W. A.	The violet (Das Veilchen) g,e
623	Old Irish Folk Melody arr. G. Nyklicek	The little red lark
624	Old English	Come, let's be merry
625	Quilter, Roger	Love's philosophy
626	Quilter, Roger	O mistress mine
627	Rachmaninoff, S.	How fair this spot (Tout est si beau) fr,e
628	Sibelius, Jean	Black roses (Svarta Rosor) nor,e
629	Vaughan Williams, R.	Silent noon

Both these volumes represent good collections of basic material.

THE ART SONG

Volume 25 of Music for Millions Series

Medium Voice

Consolidated Music Publishers, 1960

Key and Range

630 Anchieta, Juan de   Con amores, la mi madre sp

631 Bach, J. S.   Bist du bei mir g

632 Bartok, Bela   Silver moonbeams hung e

633 Beethoven, Ludwig v.   Die Ehre Gottes aud der Natur g

634 Berlioz, Hector   L'absence fr

635 Bizet, Georges   Ouvre ton coeur fr

636 Brahms, Johannes   Immer leiser wird mein Schlummer g

637 Brahms, Johannes   Mädchenlied g

638 Brahms, Johannes   Mein Mädel hat einen Rosenmund g

639 Brahms, Johannes   Sonntag g

640 Bruneau, Alfred   L'heureaux vagabond fr

55

641	Chausson, Ernest	Le temps des lilas fr
642	Delibes, Lio	Bonjour, Suzon! fr
643	Debussy, Claude	Beau soir fr
644	Debussy, Claude	Mandoline fr
645	Duparc, Henri	Extase fr
646	Durante, Francesco	Vergin, tutto amor it
647	Dvorak, Antonin	Biblical Song (Lord, Thou my Shepherd) czech,e
648	Fauré, Gabriel	Apres un rêve, fr
649	Franz, Robert	Aus meinen grossen Schmerzen g
650	Giordani, Giuseppe	Caro mio ben it
651	Granados, Enrique	El tra la la y el punteado sp
652	Gretchaninov, Alex.	Cradle Song ru, e
653	Grieg, Edvard	With a primrose, (Med en primulaveris) nor,e
654	Haydn, Joseph	A Pastoral Song (My mother bids me bind my hair) e
655	Hopkinson, Francis	My days have been so won'drous free
656	Ives, Charles	Evening

657 Johnson, Robert	Dear, do not your fair beauty wrong	
658 Lully, J. B.	Air de Philis fr	
659 MacDowell, Edward	Menie	
660 Mahler, Gustave	Liebst du um Schönheit g	
661 Mendelssohn, Felix	Auf Flügeln des Gesanges g	
662 Mendelssohn, Felix	Suleika g	
663 Moussorgsky, Modeste	Evening Prayer ru,e	
664 Mozart, W. A.	Sehnsucht nach dem Frühling g	
665 Pergolesi, Giovanni	Nina it	
666 Purcell, Henry	Man is for the woman made	
667 Respighi, Ottorino	Nebbie it	
668 Scarlatti, Allesandro	O cessate di piagarmi it	
669 Schubert, Franz	Der Wegweiser g	
670 Schubert, Franz	Frühlingsglaube g	
671 Schubert, Franz	Frühlingstraum g	
672 Schubert, Franz	Morgengruss g	

673 Schumann, Robert   Die Soldatenbraut g

674 Schumann, Robert   Ich grolle nicht g

675 Schumann, Robert   Intermezzo g

676 Schumann, Robert   Lied der Braut g

677 Strauss, Richard   Zueignung g

678 Tchaikovsky, Peter   In the midst of the ball ru,e

679 Wilbye, John   Flora gave me fairest flowers

680 Wolf, Hugo   Auf ein altes Bild g

681 Wolf, Hugo   Das verlassene Mägdlein g

682 Wolf, Hugo   Der Gärtner g

683 Wolf, Hugo   Nun wandre, Maria g

This is one of the finest collections around. In all cases,
the original languages are used, with excellent translations
in the front of the book. The literature is varied and is of
high musical quality. If ranges are compatible, students would
derive a great deal from using this collection.

G. Schirmer, Inc., 1937

Key and Range

684 Ambrose, R. S.   One sweetly solemn thought

685 Arne, Michael   The lass with the delicate air

686 Bach, J. S.   My heart ever faithful (Mein gläubiges Herze) g,e

687 Balfe, M. W.   Then you'll remember me (from "The Bohemian Girl")

688 Beethoven, Ludwig v.   I love you (Ich liebe dich) g,e

689 Bizet, Georges   Habanera (from "Carmen") fr,e

690 Bland, James   Carry me back to old Virginny

691 Böhm, Carl   Calm as the night (Still wie die Nacht) g, e

692 Borodine, A.   A dissonance

693 Brahms, Johannes   Sapphic Ode (Sapphische Ode) g,e

694 Brahms, Johannes   Cradle-song (Wiegenlied) g,e

695 Capua, E. di	My sunshine (O sole mio) it,e
696 Debussy, Claude	Evening fair (Beau Soir) fr,e
697 Deis, Carl (arr)	Song of the Volga boatmen, phoneticized Russian, e
698 Dvorak, Anton	Songs my mother taught me (Als die alte Mutter) g,e
699 Foster, Stephen	My old Kentucky home, good-night
700 Fontenailles, H. de	A resolve (Obstination) fr,e
701 Franz, Robert	Dedication (Widmung) g,e
702 Giordani, Giuseppe	Dearest believe (Caro mio ben) it,e
703 Godard, Benjamin	Lullaby (from "Jocelyn") fr,e
704 Grever, Maria	Promise, love (Júrame) sp,e
705 Grieg, Edvard	I Love you (Ich liebe dich) g,e
706 Grieg, Edvard	Solvejg's Song (Solvejgs Lied) g,e
707 Hageman, Richard	Do not go my love
708 Hahn, Reynaldo	Were my songs with wings provided (Si mes vers avaient des ailes) fr,e
709 Handel, G. F.	Where'er you walk
710 Hawthorne, Alice	Whispering hope

711 Haydn, Joseph — My mother bids me bind my hair (Bind' auf dein Haar) g,e

712 Liliuokalani, H. M. — Farewell to thee (Aloha Oe) Hawaiian,e

713 Londonderry Air — Would God I were the tender apple-blossom

714 Massenet, Jules — Elegy (Élégie) fr,e

715 Mendelssohn, Felix — O rest in the Lord (from "Elijah")

716 Molloy, J. L. — Love's old, sweet song

717 Mozart, W. A. — The violet (Das Veilchen) g,e

718 Offenbach, J. — O lovely night (Barcarolle: Belle Nuit, from "Tales of Hoffman") fr,e

719 Old English Air — Drink to me only with thine eyes

720 Old Irish Air — The last rose of summer

721 Purcell, Edward — Passing by

722 Rachmaninoff, Sergei — Lilacs g,e

723 Reichardt, Louise — When the roses bloom (Hoffnung) g,e

724 Rimsky-Korsakov, N. — A song of India (Chanson indoue, from "Sadko") f,e

725 Saint-Saens, Camille — My heart at thy sweet voice (Mon coeur s'ouvre a ta voix, from "Samson et Dalila") fr,e

726 Schubert, Franz — Ave Maria g,e,latin

61

727 Schubert, Franz | Serenade (Ständchen) g,e

728 Schumann, Robert | The two grenadiers (Die beiden Grenadiere) g,e

729 Schumann, Robert | Thou art so like a flower (Du bist wie eine Blume) g,e

730 Sinding, Christian | Sylvelin g,e

731 Strauss, Richard | All soul's day (Allerseelen) g,e

732 Strauss, Richard | To you (Zueignung) g,e

733 Sullivan, Arthur | The lost chord

734 Tchaikovsky, P. I. | One who has yearn'd, alone (Nur, wer die Sehnsucht kennt) g,e

735 Tosti, F. P. | Good-bye

736 Verdi, Giuseppe | Woman so changeable (La donna e mobile) it,e

737 Voigt, H. | Mother love

738 Wagner, Richard | Dreams (Träume) g,e

739 Yradier, S. | The dove (La Paloma) sp,e

A happy mixture of "old favorites" and excellent art-songs.
Ranges vary too much to suggest this collection for any particular
voice, but it does seem most useful for the medium high female
voice.

ART SONGS FOR SCHOOL AND STUDIO, First Year

Edited by Glenn and Spouse

Oliver Ditson, Publishers, 1930

Key and Range

Med Low   Med High

740 Bayly, Thomas   Long, long ago

741 Böhm, Carl   Still as the night (Still wie die Nacht) g,e

742 Brahms, Johannes   Cradle song (Wiegenlied) g,e

743 Cadman, Charles   The little road to Kerry

744 Calbreath, Mary E.   My love rode by

745 Clokey, Joseph   The rose

746 Dichmont, William   Such a li'l fellow

747 English Folksong   O No, John!

748 Fisher, William   Under the rose

749 Franz, Robert   Dedication (Widmung) g,e

63

750 Franz, Robert	For Music (Für Musik) g,e	
751 Franz, Robert	Out of my soul's great sadness (Aus meinen grossen Schmerzen) g,e	
752 Franz, Robert	The rose complained (Es hat die Rose sich beklagt) g,e	
753 Godard, Benjamin	Florian's song (Chanson de Florian) fr,e	
754 Grant-Schaefer, G. A.	The wind speaks	
755 Gretchaninoff, Alex.	Slumber song (Berceuse) fr,e	
756 Irish Air	My love's an arbutus	
757 Old English Air	Pretty Polly Oliver	
758 Old English Air	When love is kind	
759 Purcell, Edward	Passing by	
760 Schubert, Franz	Hedge-roses (Heiden-Röslein) g,e	
761 Schubert, Franz	Who is Sylvia? (An Silvia) g,e	
762 Schumann, Robert	The lotus flower (Die Lotosblume) g,e	
763 Schumann, Robert	Thou'rt lovely as a flower (Du bist wie eine Blume) g,e	
764 Strickland, Lily	The road to home	

ART SONGS FOR SCHOOL AND STUDIO, Second year

Edited by Glenn and Spouse

Published by Oliver Ditson Co., 1934

Key and Range

Med Low   Med High

765 Brahms, Johannes   In summer fields (Feldeinsamkeit) g,e

766 Brahms, Johannes   Love song (Minnelied) g,e

767 Brahms, Johannes   Sapphic ode (Sapphische Ode) g,e

768 Densmore, John   If God left only you

769 Fisher, William A.   I heard a cry

770 Franz, Robert   His coming (Er ist gekommen) g,e

771 Franz, Robert   I wander this summer morning (Am leuchtenden Sommer Morgen) g,e

772 Franz, Robert   Request (Bitte) g,e

773 Grieg, Edvard   Solvejg's Song (Solvejgs Lied) g,e

774 Grieg, Edvard   A swan (Ein Schwan) g,e

775 Henschel, George   No embers, nor a fire brand (duet) (Kein Feuer, keine Kohle) g,e   65

776 Jensen, Adolf	Press thy cheek against mine own
777 Manney, Charles	Consecration
778 Schubert, Franz	Ave Maria e
779 Schubert, Franz	Faith in spring e
780 Schubert, Franz	Hark! Hark! the lark
781 Schumann, Robert	'Twas in the lovely month of May (Im wunderschönen Monat Mai) g,e
782 Schumann, Robert	The two grenadiers e
783 Sinding, Christian	Sylvelin g,e
784 Strickland, Lily	My lover is a fisherman
785 Swedish Folk Song	When I was seventeen (När jag blef sjutton ar) sw,e
786 Tchaikovsky, Peter	None but the lonely heart (Nur wer die Sehnsucht kennt) g,e
787 Watts, Winter	Blue are her eyes

Note: This is a comprehensive book for the second year student. The variety in composers is good as is the material. This is a good collection to supplement a student's repertoire. It should be noted that no German words are printed for "Ave Maria", "Faith in Spring" and "The Two Grenadiers".

THE NEW IMPERIAL EDITION

SOPRANO SONGS

Boosey and Hawkes, 1953

Key and Range

788	Arne, Dr. Thomas	Where the bee sucks	
789	Bishop, Henry R.	Should he upraid	
790	Brahms, Johannes	At last (So willst du des Armen) g,e	
791	Brahms, Johannes	Lullaby (Wiegenlied) g,e	
792	Brahms, Johannes	The vain suit (Vergebliches Ständchen) g,e	
793	Campian, Thomas	So sweet is thy discourse	
794	Gibbs, C. Armstrong	Why do I love?	
795	Gounod, Charles	Without thee! (Ce que je suis sans toi) fr,e	
796	Grieg, Edvard	Solveig's song	
797	Handel, G. F.	Come beloved (Care selve) it,e	
798	Handel, G. F.	Endless pleasure, endless love	

799 Handel, G. F.	Let me wander not unseen	
800 Harty, Hamilton	A lullaby	
801 Head, Michael	The singer	
802 Henschel, George	Spring	
803 Ireland, John	I have twelve oxen	
804 Linley, Thomas	O, bid your faithful Ariel fly	
805 Liszt, Franz	The Loreley (Die Lorelei) g,e	
806 Mendelssohn, Felix	Lone and joyless (Infelice) it,e	
807 Mozart, W. A.	How calm is my spirit (Ridente la calma) it,e	
808 Pergolesi, G. B.	Gentle Shepherd (Se tu m'ami) it,e	
809 Rachmaninoff, S.	How fair this spot (Tout est si beau) fr,e	
810 Schubert, Franz	Gretchen at the spinning wheel (Gretchen am Spinnrade) g,e	
811 Schubert, Franz	The Novice (Die junge Nonne) g,e	
812 Schubert, Franz	Omnipotence (Die Allmacht) g,e	
813 Schumann, Robert	The chestnut (Der Nussbaum) g,e	
814 Schumann, Robert	He is noble, he is patient (Er, der Herrlichste von allen) g,e	

815 Schumann, Robert   Suleika's song (Lied der Suleika) g,e

816 Sullivan, Arthur   Where the bee sucks

817 Strauss, Richard   A farewell (Ich schwebe) g,e

For comment, see page 84.

THE NEW IMPERIAL EDITION

MEZZO-SOPRANO SONGS

Boosey and Hawkes, 1953

Key and Range

818 Arne, T. A.   When Daisies Pied

819 Beethoven, Ludwig, v.   Know'st Thou the Land (Kennst du das
                                    Land) g,e

820 Berlioz, Hector   The Undiscovered Country (L'ile inconnue)
                                    f,e

821 Bishop, Henry   Deep in my Heart

822 Brahms, Johannes   The Blacksmith (Der Schmied) g,e

823 Brahms, Johannes   Parting (Muss es eine Trennung) g,e

824 Brahms, Johannes   Spring's secret (Der Frühling) g,e

825 Carey, Clive   Melmillo

826 Dowland, John   Who ever thinks or hopes of love

827 Handel, G. F.   Angels ever bright and fair

828 Handel, G. F.   Dryads, Sylvans (from "Time and Truth")

70

829 Handel, G. F.	Here amid the shady woods	
830 Haydn, Joseph	My Mother bids me bind my hair	
831 Haydn, Joseph	Now the dancing sunbeams play (The Mermaid's Song)	
832 Howells, Herbert	Girls' song	
833 Mozart, W. A.	The Violet (Das Veilchen) g,e	
834 Purcell, Henry	I attempt from love's sickness to fly	
835 Purcell, Henry	Nymphs and Shepherds	
836 Quilter, Roger	Dream Valley	
837 Rachmaninoff, S.	To the Children (Aux enfants) f,e	
838 Rosa, Salvator	Let me linger near thee (Star vicino) it,e	
839 Schubert, Franz	Cradle Song (Wiegenlied) g,e	
840 Schubert, Franz	Peace (Du bist die Ruh') g,e	
841 Schubert, Franz	The Wild Rose (Heiden Röslein) g,e	
842 Schumann, Robert	The Bride's Song (Lied der Braut) g,e	
843 Schumann, Robert	Somebody (Jemand) g,e	
844 Strauss, Richard	Alone in the Forest (Waldseligkeit) g,e	

71

845 Sullivan, Arthur   Orpheus with his lute

846 Taubert, Wilhelm   In a strange land (In der Fremde) g,e

847 Wagner, Richard   Slumber Song (Dors, mon enfant) fre,e

For comment, see page 84.

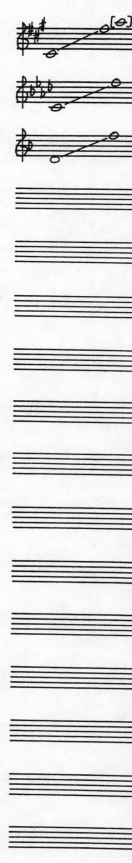

THE NEW IMPERIAL EDITION

CONTRALTO SONGS

Boosey and Hawkes, 1953

Key and Range

848 Beethoven, L. van   The praise of God (Die Ehre Gottes aus der
                             Natur) g,e

849 Brahms, Johannes   Love triumphant (Von ewiger Liebe) g,e

850 Brahms, Johannes   A night in May (Die Mainacht) g,e

851 Brahms, Johannes   Sapphic ode (Sapphische Ode) g,e

852 Britten, B. arr.   O can ye sew cushions

853 Caldara, A.   As a sunbeam at morn (Come raggio di sol)
                             it,e

854 Campian, Thomas   Oft have I sighed

855 Elgar, Edward   Where corals lie (from "Sea Pictures")

856 Gluck, C. W. von   Author of all my joys (O del mio dolce
                             ardor) it,e

857 Gounod, C.   Serenade (Quand tu chantes) fr,e

858 Handel, G. F.   Dearest consort (Cara sposa) it,e

73

859 Handel, G. F.	How changed the vision (Cangio d'aspetto) it,e	
860 Handel, G. F.	Verdant meadows (Verdi prati) it,e	
861 Harty, H.	Sea wrack	
862 Hatton, J. L.	The Enchantress	
863 Haydn, Joseph	Hark! What I tell to thee	
864 Howells, H.	O my deir hert	
865 Liszt, Franz	Mignon's song (Mignon's Lied) g,e	
866 Mendelssohn, Felix	Cradle song (Bei der Wiege) g,e	
867 Mozart, W. A.	Adieu (Addio) it,e	
868 Mozart, W. A.	With a swan-like beauty gliding (Quando miro quel bel ciglio) it,e	
869 Rachmaninoff, S.	How few the joys	
870 Scarlatti, Alessandro	Dewy violets (Le violette) it,e	
871 Scarlatti, Domenico	Like any foolish moth I fly (Qual far-falleta amante) it,e	
872 Schubert, Franz	Death and the maiden (Der Tod und das Mädchen) g,e	
873 Schubert, Franz	Litany (Litanei) g,e	
874 Schubert, Franz	To music (An die Musik) g,e	

875 Schumann, Robert   My soul is dark (Mein Herz ist schwer)
                                     g,e

876 Sullivan, Arthur   The willow song

877 Tschaikowsky, P.   Nay, though my heart should break (Nur
                                     wer die Sehnsucht kennt) g,e

For comment, see page 84.

THE NEW IMPERIAL EDITION

TENOR SONGS

Boosey and Hawkes, 1953

Key and Range

878 Arne, Thomas A.   Under the greenwood tree

879 Beethoven, Ludwig   Adelaide g,e

880 Brahms, Johannes   Is it bliss or is it sorrow
                             (Sind es Schmerzen, sind es Freuden?) g,e

881 Brahms, Johannes   Love song (Minnelied) g,e

882 Brahms, Johannes   Reign here a Queen within the heart
                             (Wie bist du, meine Königin) g,e

883 Bridge, Frank   E'en as a lovely flower

884 Caccini, Giulio   Amarylis it,e

885 Elgar, Edward   Is she not passing fair?

886 Gurney, Ivor   Sleep

887 Handel, G. F.   Where e'er you walk

888 Handel, G. F.   Would you gain the tender creature

76

889 Handel, G. F.	Ye verdant hills	
890 Loder, Edward	The brooklet	
891 Mendelssohn, Felix	On wings of song (Auf Flügeln des Gesanges) g,e	
892 Pilkington, Francis	Rest, sweet nymphs	
893 Purcell, Henry	I'll sail upon the Dog-star	
894 Purcell, Henry	The knotting song	
895 Quilter, Roger	Now sleeps the crimson petal	
896 Rachmaninoff, Serge	Night is mournful (L'ombre est triste) f,e	
897 Schubert, Franz	The secret (Geheimes) g,e	
898 Schubert, Franz	Whither? (Wohin?) g,e	
899 Schubert, Franz	Who is Sylvia? (An Silvia) g,e	
900 Schumann, Robert	Moonlight (Mondnacht) g,e	
901 Schumann, Robert	Thou'rt like a lovely flower (Du bist wie eine Blume) g,e	
902 Stevens, R. J. S.	Sigh no more, ladies	
903 Strauss, Richard	A winter dedication (Winterweihe) g,e	
904 Tchaikowsky, Peter	'Twas April	

77

905 Vaughan Williams, R.   From far, from eve and morning (from
                             "On Wenlock Edge")

906 Warlock, Peter   As ever I saw

907 White, Maud Valerie   To Mary

       For comment, see page 84.

THE NEW IMPERIAL EDITION
BARITONE SONGS
Boosey and Hawkes, 1953

Key and Range

908 Arne, Thomas   The plague of love

909 Beethoven, Ludwig   To the faithless one (Als die Geliebte
                                sich trennen wollte) g,e

910 Brahms, Johannes   The garland (Die Kränze) g,e

911 Brahms, Johannes   The message (Die Botschaft) g,e

912 Brahms, Johannes   Sunday morning (Sonntag) g,e

913 Dowland, John   Come again, sweet love

914 Gurney, Ivor   The bonnie Earl of Murray

915 Handel, G. F.   How art thou fall'n

916 Handel, G. F.   Revenge! Timotheus cries

917 Handel, G. F.   Thrice happy the monarch

918 Hatton, J. L.   To Anthea

919 Loewe, Carl	Edward g,e	
920 Purcell, Henry	Let the dreadful engines	
921 Purcell, Henry	Ye twice ten hundred deities	
922 Quilter, Roger	O mistress mine	
923 Rachmaninoff, S.	When yesterday we met (Je la vis s'arreter) fr,e	
924 Scarlatti, Alessandro	Cease, oh maiden (O Cessate) it,e	
925 Schubert, Franz	The Erl King (Der Erlkönig) g,e	
926 Schubert, Franz	The wanderer (Der Wanderer) g,e	
927 Schubert, Franz	The wraith (Der Doppelgänger) g,e	
928 Schumann, Robert	Belshazzar (Belsatzar) g,e	
929 Schumann, Robert	Thy lovely face (Dein Angesicht) g,e	
930 Schumann, Robert	Why blame thee now? (Ich grolle nicht)g,e	
931 Somervell, Arthur	Birds in the high hall-garden	
932 Strauss, Richard	A welcome vision (Freundliche Vision) g,e	
933 Sullivan, Arthur	If doughty deeds my lady please	
934 Tchaikowsky, P. I.	Don Juan's Serenade	

935 Warlock, Peter   Walking in the woods

936 White, Maud Valerie   King Charles

937 Vaughan Williams, R.   Youth and Love

      For comment, see page 84.

THE NEW IMPERIAL EDITION

BASS SONGS

Boosey and Hawkes, 1953

Key and Range

938 Arne, Thomas A.   Bacchus, God of mirth and wine

939 Beethoven, Ludwig   The song of the flea (Es war einmal
                             ein König) g,e

940 Blow, Dr. John   The self-banished

941 Brahms, Johannes   Earth and sky (Feldeinsamkeit) g,e

942 Brahms, Johannes   I said I will forget thee (Nicht mehr
                             zu dir zu gehen) g,e

943 Buononcini, G. B.   Love leads to battle (Pupille nere) it,e

944 Carissimi, G.   I triumph! I triumph! (Vittoria!
                             Vittoria!) it,e

945 English Air   Down among the dead men

946 German "Trinklied"   Drinking

947 Gounod, Charles   The Valley (Le Vallon) f,e

948 Handel, G. F.	Droop not young lover		
949 Handel, G. F.	Love that's true will live forever (Si, tra i ceppi) it,e		
950 Harty, Hamilton (arr)	My lagan love		
951 Head, Michael	Money, O!		
952 Hume, T.	Tobacco		
953 Lully, J. B.	All your shades (Bois epais) fr,e		
954 Mendelssohn, Felix	I am a roamer		
955 Mozart, W. A.	Thoughts at even-tide (Abendempfindung) g,e		
956 Purcell, Henry	Arise, ye subterranean winds		
957 Purcell, Henry	Hear! Ye Gods of Britain		
958 Purcell, Henry	The owl is abroad		
959 Rachmaninoff, S.	By the grave		
960 Schubert, Franz	The lay of the imprisoned huntsman (Lied des gefangenen Jägers) g,e		
961 Schubert, Franz	The lime-tree (Der Lindenbaum) g,e		
962 Schubert, Franz	My last abode (Aufenthalt) g,e		
963 Schumann, Robert	The Last Toast (Auf das Trinkglass) g,e		

964 Schumann, Robert   The two grenadiers (Die beiden Grenadiere)
                          g,e

965 Strauss, Richard   The solitary one (Der Einsame) g,e

966 Tschaikowsky, P. I.   To the forest

967 Wood, Charles   Ethiopia saluting the colours

These volumes have been available for a number of years and
represent a novel idea: a separate collection for each of six
voices. I think there is much of value in each, most in the
category of intermediate to advanced. They are worth having.

THE SINGING ROAD, VOL. I

Compiled and Edited by Arthur Ward

Carl Fischer, Inc., 1939

Key and Range

968 Bach, J. S.	If thou thy heart wilt give me	
969 Brahms, Johannes	Lullaby (Wiegenlied) g, e	
970 Crist, Bainbridge	Blue bird	
971 deFontainailles, H	A resolve (Obstination)fr, e	
972 Foster, Stephen	Beautiful dreamer	
973 Fox, Oscar	I'll never ask you to tell	
974 Franz, Robert	Dedication (Widmung)g, e	
975 Giordani, Tommaso	Dearest and best (Caro mio ben)it,e	
976 Goetze, Carl	O happy day! (O schöne Zeit)g,e	
977 Handel, G. F.	Where'er you walk	
978 Horn, Charles	Cherry ripe	

85

979 Horrocks, Amy   The bird and the rose

980 Kjerulf, Halfdan   Last night

981 Mozart, W. A.   Lullaby

982 Old English Folk-song Drink to me only with thine eyes

983 Old Scotch Melody arr. Loch Lomond
    Crist

984 Richardson, T.   Mary

985 Rubenstein, Anton   Thou'rt like unto a flower (Du
bist wie eine Blume)g, e

986 Schubert, Franz   Morning greeting (Morgengruss)g,e

987 Schubert, Franz   To Music (An die Musik) g, e

988 Schumann, Robert   Folk-song (Volksliedchen) g, e

This volume, for beginning students, has some interesting
features: In addition to having a good choice of songs
(several not found in any other volume), it also has
excellent background material for each song, and Vaccai
exercises interspersed throughout.

THE SINGING ROAD, VOL. II

Compiled and Edited by Arthur Ward

Carl Fischer, Inc., 1950

Key and Range
Med Low   Med High

989 Anonymous   Have you seen but the whyte lillie
                         grow

990 Arne, Thomas   The lass with the delicate air

991 Bach, J. S.   Come sweet repose

992 Handel, G. F.   O sleep why dost thou leave me

993 Haydn, Joseph   My mother bids me bind my hair

994 Mozart, W. A.   The violet (Das Veilchen)g, e

995 Pergolesi, Giovanni Nina, it, e

996 Tosti, Francesco   Could I (Vorrei) it, e

· 997 Tosti, Francesco   Serenade (La Serenata)it, e

87

THE SINGING ROAD, VOL. III

Compiled and Edited by Arthur Ward

Carl Fischer, Inc., 1950

Key and Range
Med Low   Med High

998 Beethoven, L. van   I love thee (Ich liebe dich)g, e

999 Brahms, Johannes   Sapphic ode (Sapphische Ode)g, e

1000 Fox, Oscar   My heart is a silent violin

1001 Grieg, Edvard   I love thee

1002 Lassen, Eduard   Thine eyes so blue

1003 Massenet, Jules   Open thy blue eyes (Ouvre tes yeux
                             bleus)fr, e

1004 Schubert, Franz   Serenade (Ständchen)g, e

1005 Schumann, Robert   When gazing in thine eyes so dear
                             (Wenn ich in deine Augen seh')g,e

1006 Ward, Arthur   The purple orchard

As with Volume I, the songs in volumes II and III are well-
chosen, alittle longer and more difficult. They also have
introductory paragraphs , and each volume has different
Marchesi exercises. Prices vary.

WORLD'S FAVORITE ART SONGS

OF THREE CENTURIES

Ashley Publications, Inc., 1976

Key and Range

1007 Brahms, Johannes   A thought like music (Wie Melodien zieht es mir)g, e

1008 Cornelius, Peter   The monotone (Ein Ton)g, e

1009 D'Hardelot, Guy   Because (Berceuse)fr,e

1010 Dvorak, Anton   Songs my mother taught me(Als die alte Mutter) g, e

1011 Faure, Jean B.   The palms (Les paumes) fr, e

1012 Franz, Robert   Delight of Melancholy (Wonne der Wehmuth)g, e

1013 Godard, Benjamin   Florian's song (Chanson de Florian)fr, e

1014 Gounod, Charles   Entreat me not to leave thee, e

1015 Grieg, Edvard   At the brookside (An einem Bache) g, e

1016 Grieg, Edvard   The first primrose (Mit einer primula veris) g, e

1017 Grieg, Edvard   From Monte Pincio (Von Monte Pincio) g,e

1018 Grieg, Edvard   I love thee (Ich liebe dich)g, e

1019 Handel, G. F.   Come, my beloved (Care selve)it, e

1020 Hildach, Eugen   Spring, (Lenz) g

1021 Humperdinck, E.   Now I lay me down to sleep (Abends, will ich schlafen gehn)g, e

1022 Liszt, Franz   The king of Thule (Der König von Thule)g, e

1023 Liszt, Franz   Wanderer's night song (Wanderers Nachtlied)g,e

1024 Massenet, Jules   Elegy (Élégie)fr, e

1025 Mozart, W. A.   The violet (Das Veilchen)g, e

1026 Puccini, G.   Her own place (In quelle trine morbide)it, e

1027 Puccini, G.   Musetta's waltz,(Quando m'en vo)it,e

1028 Puccini, G.   One fine day (Un bel di)it, e

1029 Puccini, G.   They call me Mimi (Mi chiamano Mimi)it, e

1030 Saint-Saëns, C.   My heart at thy sweet voice (Mon coeur s'ouvre a ta voix)fr, e

1031 Schubert, Franz   Flutterby (Blanka)g, e

1032 Schubert, Franz   The joy of tears (Wonne der Wehmuth)g, e

1033 Schubert, Franz   Life's a carousel (Irdisches Glück)g,

90

1034 Schubert, Franz	Moonshine (Klage an den Mond)g
1035 Schubert, Franz	Of God and man (Grenzen der Menschheit) g
1036 Schumann, Robert	Dedication (Widmung) g, e
1037 Schumann, Robert	No tears (Ich grolle nicht)g, e
1038 Strauss, Richard	Serenade (Ständchen)g, e
1039 Tschaikovsky, P.	Disappointment (Deception)fr, e
1040 Tschaikovsky, P.	None but the lonely heart (Nur wer die Sehnsucht kennt)g, e
1041 Tschaikovsky, P.	Why (Warum?)g, e
1042 Wolf, Hugo	A bouquet (Blumengruss)g, e
1043 Wolf, Hugo	The gardener (Der Gärtner)g, e
1044 Wolf, Hugo	The Meeting (Begegnung) g, e
1045 Wolf, Hugo	Morning (In der Frühe)g, e
1046 Wolf, Hugo	Questions and answers (Frage und Antwort)g, e
1047 Wolf, Hugo	The suitor (Ständchen)g, e
1048 Wagner, Richard	Dreams (Träume)g, e
1049 Wagner, Richard	Lullaby (Dors, mon enfant)fr, e

This is a disappointing collection, especially in the editing. I
was also bothered by the fact that some songs have English texts
in the music, others only in translation that precedes the song.
The price (at this writing $5.95) might make up for some of the
above criticisms. This collection does have a number of fine
songs, some of which are not found in other collections. Ranges
are, for the most part, for high voice.

GREAT ART SONGS OF THREE CENTURIES

Compiled by Bernard Taylor

G. Schirmer, Inc., 1960

		Key and Range
		Low — High
1050 Alvarez, Fermin M.	The Farewell (La Partida)sp, e	
1051 Bachelet, Alfred	Dearest night (Chère nuit)fr, e	
1052 Beethoven, L. van	Joyful and woeful (Freudvoll und Leidvoll)g, e	
1053 Beethoven, L. van	New love, new life (Neue Liebe, Neues Leben) g, e	
1054 Berlioz, Hector	Absence, fr, e	
1055 Bononcini, Giovanni	For the love my heart doth prize (Per la gloria d'adorarvi)it, e	
1056 Brahms, Johannes	The huntsman (Der Jäger)g, e	
1057 Brahms, Johannes	The May night (Die Mainacht)g, e	
1058 Brahms, Johannes	The message (Botschaft)g, e	
1059 Brahms, Johannes	My songs (Meine Lieder)g, e	
1060 Brahms, Johannes	Serenade (Ständchen)g, e	

93

1061 Chausson, Ernest	The butterflies (Les papillons)fr, e	
1062 Debussy, Claude	Field Flowers (Fleur des Blés)fr, e	
1063 Debussy, Claude	Lovely night of stars (Nuit d'étoiles) fr, e	
1064 Debussy, Claude	Moonlight (Clair de lune)fr, e	
1065 deLuca, S.	I do not dare despond (Non posso disperar)it, e	
1066 Fauré, Gabriel	Aurora (Aurore)fr, e	
1067 Fauré, Gabriel	Here below (Ici-bas!)fr, e	
1068 Fauré, Gabriel	In the ruins of an abbey (Dans les ruines d'une abbaye)fr, e	
1069 Ferrari, Gustave	The mirror (Le miroir)fr, e	
1070 Grieg, Edvard	Eros, g, e	
1071 Grieg, Edvard	Spring (Vaaren)nor, e	
1072 Hahn, Reynaldo	From a prison (D'une prison)fr, e	
1073 Hahn, Reynaldo	Offering (Offrande)fr, e	
1074 Handel, G. F.	Howsoever they may revile me (Si, tra i ceppi)it, e	
1075 Handel, G. F.	Leave me, loathsome light	
1076 Handel, G. F.	Praise be to Thee (Dank sei Dir, Herr) g, e	

1077	Handel, G. F.	Te Deum (Vouchsafe, O Lord) e	
1078	Handel, G. F.	Where now art thou, my own (Dove sei, amato bene?) it,e	
1079	Haydn, Joseph	Life is a dream (Das Leben ist ein Traum) g,e	
1080	Haydn, Joseph	She never told her love, e	
1081	Leoncavallo, R.	Wake with the dawn (Mattinata) it,e	
1082	Mattei, Tito	'Tis not true (Non'e ver) it,e	
1083	Monteverdi, Claudio	No longer let me languish (Lasciatemi morire) it,e	
1084	Moussorgsky, Modest	The Seminarian, e	
1085	Moussorgsky, Modest	The song of Khivria	
1086	Pierné, Gabriel	Boat song (En barque) fr,e	
1087	Purcell, Henry	Nymphs and shepherds	
1088	Rachmaninoff, Sergei	Forsake me not, my love I pray, e	
1089	Rachmaninoff, Sergei	To the children, e	
1090	Rachmaninoff, Sergei	Vocalise	
1091	Sandoval, Miguel	Gypsy serenade (Serenata Gitana) sp,e	
1092	Sandoval, Miguel	Without your love (Sin tu amor) sp,e	

1093 Scarlatti, A.	The violets (Le violette) it,e	
1094 Schubert, Franz	The Butterfly (Der Schmetterling) g,e	
1095 Schubert, Franz	Impatience (Ungeduld) g,e	
1096 Schubert, Franz	To the lyre (An die Leier) g,e	
1097 Schubert, Franz	With you (Bei dir) g,e	
1098 Schumann, Robert	Hidden tears (Stille Tränen) g,e	
1099 Schumann, Robert	Messages (Aufträge) g,e	
1100 Schumann, Robert	Sunday on the Rhine (Sonntags am Rhein) g,e	
1101 Schumann, Robert	Thine image pure (Intermezzo) g,e	
1102 Sgambati, Giovanni	Parting (Separazione) it,e	
1103 Strauss, Richard	Homecoming (Heimkehr) g,e	
1104 Strauss, Richard	Your eyes so blue and tender (Mit deinen blauen Augen) g,e	
1105 Wolf, Hugo	Farewell (Lebe wohl) g,e	
1106 Wolf, Hugo	From her balcony green (Auf dem grünen Balcon) g,e	
1107 Wolf, Hugo	Go forth now, sweet Mary (Nun wandre Maria) g,e	
1108 Wolf, Hugo	Insatiable love (Nimmersatte Liebe) g,e	

CLASSIC SONGS: ITALIAN, FRENCH, ENGLISH

Compiled and Edited by Bernard Taylor

Summy-Birchard, 1959

Reprinted with permission by Frangipani Press, n.d.

Key and Range

Low   High

1109 Carissimi, Giacomo   I cannot live alone (Non posso
                                 vivere) it,e

1110 English Folk Song   Come let's be merry
        arr. Wilson

1111 English Folk Song   The happy lover
        arr. Wilson

1112 Fifteenth-century Song   My heart is glad (L'amour de moi)
                                 fr,e

1113 Handel, G. F.   Solace to my heart (Sorge nel
                                 petto) it,e

1114 Lully, Jean-Babtiste   Gloomy woods (Bois épais) fr,e

1115 Monro, George   My lovely Celia

1116 Rousseau, J. J.   The rose-tree (Le Rosier) fr,e
        arr. Weckerlin

1117 Scarlatti, Alessandro   O, sweet hope (O, dolcissima
                                 speranza) it,e

1118 Song of Alsace   The morning star (L'étoile du
        arr. Weckerlin   matin) fr,e

1119 Stradella, Alessandro   Now be merry and gay (Se nel ben)
                                 it,e

1120 Vivaldi, Antonio Crying, weeping (Piango gemo)
           it,e

1121 Young, Anthony Phillis has such charming graces

A good collection for a younger student. It might also
serve as class voice material. I'm glad to see this back
in print.

ITALIAN SONGS OF THE 18th CENTURY

Medium Voice

International Music Company, 1954

Key and Range

1122 Bononcini, Giovanni   La speranza i cori affida

1123 Bononcini, Giovanni   Lungi da te

1124 Bononcini, Giovanni   Piu vaga e vezzosetta

1125 Bononcini, Giovanni   Se ti piace

1126 Caldara, Antonio   Si t'intendo

1127 Fedeli, Ruggiero   Il mio core

1128 Hasse, Giovanni   Voi che credete

1129 Mancini, Francesco   Dir ch'io t'ami

1130 Manzi, Luigi   Hai core, o crudele

1131 Marcello, Benedetto   Lontananza e gelosia

1132 Marcello, Benedetto   Vedi quel ruscelletto

1133 Maria Antonia (E.T.P.A.) Prendi l'ultimo addio

1134 Perti, Giacomo Begli occhi

1135 Perti, Giacomo Dolce, scherza

1136 Pignatta, Giuseppe Cieco se finse amor

1137 Porpora, Niccolo Come la luce è tremola

1138 Scarlatti, Alessandro Nevi intatte

1139 Scarlatti, Alessandro Per formare la Betta

1140 Scarlatti, Alessandro Va per lo mare

1141 Torelli, Giuseppe Tu lo sai

This is an excellent collection of Italian songs for medium
voice. Although there is no singing translation in English,
each poem is translated at the start of the song.

ANTHOLOGY OF ITALIAN SONG

of the 17th and 18th Centuries

Book 1

G. Schirmer Inc., 1922

Key and Range

1142 Bononcini, G. M.   Ah! why let me ever languish
                               (Deh piu a me non v'ascondete)

1143 Caldara, A.   As on the swelling wave (Come raggio di sol)

1144 Caldara, A.   Kindly forest (Selve amiche)

1145 Caldara, A.   Tho' not deserving (Sebben crudele)

1146 Carissimi, G. G.   Victorious my heart is (Vittoria, vittoria!)

1147 Cesti, M. A.   Caressing mine idol's pillow
                               (Intorno all'idol mio)

1148 Gluck, C.   O thou belov'd (O del mio dolce ardor)

1149 Handel, G. F.   Ah, poor heart (Ah! mio cor)

1150 Handel, G. F.   O agonies of thought (Affanni del pensier)

1151 Jomelli, N.   Oh! who will buy (Chi vuol comprar)

1152 Legrenzi, G.   How void of compassion (Che fiero costume)

101

1153 Lotti, A.	Mouth so charmful (Pur dicesti, bocca bella)
1154 Marcello, B.	In my heart the flames (Quella fiamma che m'accende)
1155 Martini, G.	The joys of love (Piacer d'amor)
1156 Paisiello, G.	When, my love, wilt thou return (Il mio ben quando verra)
1157 Paisiello, G.	Who'll try the Gypsy pretty (Chi vuol la zingarella)
1158 Paisiello, G.	Why feels my heart so dormant (Nel cor piu non mi sento)
1159 Pergolesi, G. B.	All of anguish most unsparing (Ogni pena piu spietata
1160 Pergolesi, G. B.	If thou lov'st me (Se tu m'ami, se sospiri)
1161 Pergolesi, G. B.	Unruly, Sir, unruly (Stizzoso, mio stizzoso)
1162 Piccinni, N.	O night, mysterious goddess (O notte, o Dea) fr,it,e
1163 Scarlatti, A.	Desponding, lonely (Son tutta duolo)
1164 Scarlatti, A.	Oft the blind-fold boy (Spesso vibra per suo gioco)
1165 Scarlatti, A.	O no longer seek to pain me (O cessate di piagarmi)
1166 Scarlatti, A.	Should Florindo be faithful (Se Florindo e fedele)
1167 Scarlatti, A.	Wouldst thou the boast of ending (Se tu della mia morte)
1168 Scarlatti, D.	Take heart again (Consolati e spera)

1169 Traetta, T.   Gentle shade, well beloved (Ombra cara, amorosa)

1170 Vivaldi, A.   There's one, I know him not (Un certo non so che)

This volume has both Italian and English texts for each song.

ANTHOLOGY OF ITALIAN SONG OF THE 17th AND 18th

CENTURIES Book 2

G. Schirmer, Inc., 1926

Key and Range

1171 Bassani, G. B.   Art thou sleeping, fair one (Dormi, bella dormi tu?) it,e

1172 Bassani, G. B.   Mourn with temerity (Seguita a piangere) it, e

1173 Bassani, G. B.   Sleep on, then (Posate, dormite) it,e

1174 Bononcini, G. B.   For the love my heart doth prize (Per la gloria d'adorarvi) it,e

1175 Caccini, G.   Amarilli, my fair one (Amarilli, mia bella) it,e

1176 Cavalli, F.   Ye blisses, that ravish (Delizie contente) it, e

1177 Cesti, M. A.   Wilt no longer thou torment me (Tu mancavi a tormentarmi) it,e

1178 Del Leuto, A.   Tell me, Love (Dimmi, Amor) it,e

1179 De Luca, S.   I do not dare despond (Non posso disperar) it, e

1180 Durante, F.   Dance, o dance, maiden gay (Danza, danza fanciulla gentile) it, e

1181 Durante, F.   Virgin, fount of love (Vergin tutto amor) it, e

104

1182 Falconieri, A.   Charming eyes so wary (Vezzosette e care) it, e

1183 Fasolo, G. B.   Change, o change thy fond wishes (Cangia, cangia tue voglie) it, e

1184 Gasparini, F.   Dainty meshes, net enticeful (Caro laccio, dolce nodo) it,e

1185 Gasparini, F.   Love's bond to sever (Lasciar d'amarti) it,e

1186 Giordani, G.   Thou all my bliss (Caro mio ben) it,e

1187 Marcello, B.   For my love thus to die (Non m'e grave morir per amore) it,e

1188 Monteverdi, C.   No longer let me languish (Lasciatemi morire) it,e

1189 Paradies, P. D.   'Tis love, that rogue so wily (M'ha preso alla sua ragna) it,e

1190 Piccinni, N.   Since Heaven has torn me (Se il ciel me divide) it,e

1191 Rontani, R.   When the murm'ring (Se bel rio) it,e

1192 Sarri, D.   As when a lamb confiding (Sen corre l'agnelletta) it,e

1193 Scarlatti, A.   Hey, come hither, ye fancies (Su, venite a consiglio) it,e

1194 Scarlatti, A.   My heart doth languish (Sento nel core) it,e

1195 Scarlatti, A.   O'er Ganges now launches (Gia il sole dal Gange) it,e

1196 Scarlatti, A.   To win glory (All'acquisto di gloria) it,e

1197 Stradella, A.   How dearly are prized (Ragion sempre addita) it,e

1198 Stradella, A.   If love my feet enchaineth (Se amor
                            m'annoda il piede) it,e

1199 Tenaglia, A. F.   O when will ye e'er leave me (E quando ve
                            n'andate) it,e

1200 Tenaglia, A. F.   When will the day e'er be (Quando sara
                            quel di) it,e

24 ITALIAN SONGS AND ARIAS

OF THE 17th and 18th CENTURIES

Published by G. Schirmer, Inc., 1948

Key and Range

Med Low   Med High

1201 Bononcini, G. B.   For the love my heart doth prize (Per la gloria d'adoravi) it,e

1202 Caccini, G.   Amarilli, my fair one (Amarilli, mia bella) it,e

1203 Caldara, Antonio   As on the swelling wave (Come raggio di sol) it,e

1204 Caldara, Antonio   Fairest adored (Alma del core) it,e

1205 Caldara, Antonio   Tho' not deserving (Sebben crudele) it,e

1206 Carissimi, G.   Victorious my heart is (Vittoria, mio core) it,e

1207 DeLuca, S.   I do not dare despond (Non posso disperar) it,e

1208 Durante, F.   Dance, O dance, maiden gay (Danza, danza fanciulla gentile) it,e

1209 Durante, F.   Virgin, fount of love (Vergin, tutto amor) it,e

1210 Giordani, G.   Thou all my bliss (Caro mio ben) it,e

1211 Gluck, C. W. von   O thou belov'd (O del mio dolce ardor) it,e

107

1212 Legrenzi, G.	How void of compassion (Che fiero costume) it,e	
1213 Lotti, A.	Mouth so charmful (Pur dicesti, o bocca bella) it,e	
1214 Marcello, B.	My joyful ardor (Il mio bel foco) it,e	
1215 Monteverdi, C.	No longer let me languish (Lasciatemi morire!) it,e	
1216 Paisiello, G.	Why feels my heart so dormant (Nel cor piu non mi sento) it,e	
1217 Pergolesi, G. B.	If thou lov'st me (Se tu m'ami, se sospiri) it,e	
1218 Pergolesi, G. B.	Nina it,e	
1219 Scarlatti, Alessandro	O'er Ganges now launches (Gia sole dal Ganges) it,e	
1220 Scarlatti, Alessandro	O no longer seek to pain me (O cessate di piagarmi) it,e	
1221 Scarlatti, Alessandro	Should Florindo be faithful (Se Florindo e fedele) it,e	
1222 Scarlatti, Alessandro	The violets (Le violette) it,e	
1223 Stradella, A.	O Lord, have mercy (Pieta, Signore) it,e	
1224 Torelli, G.	Ask thy heart (Tu lo sai) it,e	

WORLD'S FAVORITE ITALIAN SONGS AND ARIAS

OF THE 17th AND 18th CENTURIES

Ashley Publications, Inc., 1981

Key and Range

1225 Bononcini, Giovanni   For the love my heart doth prize (Per la gloria d'adorarvi) it, e

1226 Bononcini, Giovanni   Lungi da te, it

1227 Bononcini, Giovanni   Se ti piace, it

1228 Caccini, Giulio   Amarilli, my fair one (Amarilli, mia bella) it, e

1229 Caldara, Antonio   As on the swelling wave (Come raggio di sol) it, e

1230 Caldara, Antonio   Fairest adored (Alma del core) it, e

1231 Caldara, Antonio   Si t'intendo, it

1232 Caldara, Antonio   Tho' not deserving (Sebben crudele) it,e

1233 Carissimi, Giacomo   Victorious my heart is (Vittoria, mio core) it, e

1234 De Luca, S.   I do not dare despond (Non posso disperar) it, e

1235 Durante, Francesco   Dance, o dance, maiden gay (Danza, danza fanciulla gentile) it, e

1236	Durante, Francesco	Virgin, fount of love (Vergin, tutto amor) it, e	
1237	Giordani, Giuseppe	Thou, all my bliss (Caro mio ben) it, e	
1238	Gluck, C. W. von	O thou belov'd (O del mio dolce ardor)it,e	
1239	Hasse, Giovanni	Voi che credete, it	
1240	Legrenzi, Giovanni	How void of compassion (Che fiero costume) it, e	
1241	Lotti, Antonio	Mouth so charmful (Pur dicesti, o bocca bella) it, e	
1242	Mancini, Francesco	Dir ch'io t'ami, it	
1243	Marcello, Benedetto	My joyful ardor (Il mio bel foco) it, e	
1244	Marcello, Benedetto	Vedi quel ruscelletto, it	
1245	Monteverdi, Claudio	No longer let me languish (Lasciatemi morire) it, e	
1246	Paisiello, Giovanni	Why feels my heart so dormant (Nel cor piu non mi sento) it, e	
1247	Pergolesi, Giovanni	If thou lov'st me (Se tu m'ami, se sospiri) it, e	
1248	Pergolesi, Giovanni	Nina, it, e	
1249	Perti, G. A.	Dolce scherza, it	
1250	Pignatta, Giuseppe	Cieco si finse amor, it	
1251	Scarlatti, Alessandro	Nevi intatte, it	

1252 Scarlatti, A.	O no longer seek to pain me (O cessate di piagarmi) it, e	
1253 Scarlatti, A.	O'er Ganges now launches (Gia il sole dal Gange) it, e	
1254 Scarlatti, A.	Per formare la Betta, it	
1255 Scarlatti, A.	Should Florindo be faithful (Se Florindo e fedele) it, e	
1256 Scarlatti, A.	Va per lo mare, it	
1257 Scarlatti, A.	The violets (Le violette) it, e	
1258 Stradella, Alessandro	O Lord, have mercy (Pieta, Signore)it, e	
1259 Torelli, Giuseppe	Ask thy heart (Tu lo sai) it, e	

An excellent collection of 35 Italian songs, some with English translations with the music, others with an English translation preceding the song. For the price (at this writing, $5.95) an outstanding value, if the voice fits the ranges.

CLASSIC ITALIAN SONGS, Vol. I

Edited by Mabelle Glenn and Bernard Taylor

Oliver Ditson Company, 1936

Key and Range

Med Low   Med High

1260 Bencini, Pietro   E'er will I sigh (Tanto sospirero)
it, e

1261 Caccini, Giulio   Amaryllis (Amarilli),it, e

1262 Carissimi, G.   No, no, hope has perished (No, no,
non si speri)it, e

1263 Carissimi, G.   Victorious, my heart (Vittoria, mio
core)it, e

1264 Cavalli, Francesco   Oh, hasten, ye maidens (Donzelle
fuggite)it, e

1265 Durante, Francesco   Virgin, full of grace (Vergin, tutto
amor)it,e

1266 Frescobaldi, G.   When soft the breezes (Se l'aura
spira)it, e

1267 Giordani, Giuseppe   My dearest love (Caro mio ben)it, e

1268 Lotti, Antonio   Speak again, love (Pur dicesti, o
bocca bella)it, e

1269 Monteverdi, C.   Alas, all too harsh and ruthless (Ahi,
troppo e duro)it, e

1270 Monteverdi, C.   Let death now come (Lasciatemi morire)
it,e   112

1271 Pergolesi, G. 'Tis three long days (Nina) it,e,g

1272 Peri, Jacopo Invocation of Orpheus (Invocazione de Orfeo)it, e

1273 Rosa, Salvator Forest, thy green arbors (Selve, voi che le speranze)it, e

1274 Scarlatti, Aless. Cease to torment (O cessate di piagarmi)it, e

1275 Scarlatti, Aless. Early blowing, violets growing (Rugiadose, odorose)it, e

1276 Secchi, Antonio When far from my dear treasure (Lungi dal caro bene)it, e

1277 Torelli, Giuseppe Well thou knowest (Tu lo sai)it, e

Taken altogether, the three volumes in this series represent a wonderful body of literature. Each volume has some helpful material on learning songs, Italian pronunciation, and notes on the songs. A good basic library, or supplement to other collections.

CLASSIC ITALIAN SONGS, Vol. II

Edited by Mabelle Glenn and Bernard Taylor

Oliver Ditson Company, 1949

Key and Range

Med Low   Med High

1278 Bononcini, G. B.   The wise sailor steering
                               (L'esperto nocchiero) it,e

1279 Caldara, Antonio   Heart of my own heart (Alma
                               del core) it,e

1280 Caldara, Antonio   Like the sun's golden ray (Come
                               raggio di sol) it,e

1281 Carissimi, G.   Pray, let me, suffering (Deh,
                               contentatevi) it,e

1282 Cesti, Marcantonio   Cupid can never (Ah! quanto è
                               vero) it,e

1283 Cesti, Marcantonio   Oh, whither art roaming (E dove
                               t'aggiri) it,e

1284 Durante, Francesco   Dance, O dance gentle maiden
                               (Danza, danza fanciulla gentile)
                               it,e

1285 Falconieri, Andrea   Locks so beautiful (O bellissimi
                               capelli) it,e

1286 Legrenzi, Giovanni   What strange whim pursuing (che
                               fiero costume) it,e

1287 Mazzaferrata, G. B.   Swift my heart surrenders (Presto,
                               presto io m'innamore) it,e

1288 Provenzale, Francesco   O restore to me (Deh, rendetemi)
                               it,e   114

1289 Rosa, Salvator	To be near the fair idol (Star vicino) it,e	
1290 Scarlatti, A.	I wish naught but to survey thee (Non vogl'io se non vederti) it,e	
1291 Scarlatti, A.	Loving, I borrow (Sento nel core) it,e	
1292 Stradella, Aless.	I would spend my blood unheeding (Col mio sangue comprerei) it,e	

CLASSIC ITALIAN SONGS, VOL. III

Edited by Mabelle Glenn and Bernard Taylor

Oliver Ditson Company, 1968

Key and Range

Med Low   Med High

1293 Bononcini, Giovanni   Oh, those charming lights (Deh piu
                              a me non v'ascondete)it, e

1294 Caldara, Antonio   Friendly forest (Selve amiche,
                              ombrose piante)it, e

1295 Carissimi, Giacomo   Phyllis, no more (Filli, non t'amo
                              piu)it, e

1296 Falconieri, Andrea   Ruby portal, fair, beguiling (Bella
                              porta di rubini)it, e

1297 Gaffi, Bernardo   Eyes so alluring (Luci vezzose)it,e

1298 Paisiello, Giovanni   No more my heart is fervent (Nel
                              cor piu non mi sento)it, e

1299 Pergolesi, Giovanni   If thou lov'st me (Se tu m'ami)it,e

1300 Perti, Jacopo   I yielded without repenting (Begli
                              occhi, io non me pento)it, e

1301 Scarlatti, Alessandro   The man who would turn lover (Chi
                              vuole innamorarsi)it, e

1302 Stradella, Alessandro   I languish, love, thy weary slave
                              (Cosi, amor, mi fai languir)it,e

1303 Stradella, A.   O have pity (Per pieta) it, e

116

1304 Strozzi, Barbara   Love sleeping (Amor dormiglione) it, e

1305 Traetta, Tommaso   Gentle spirit, well beloved (Ombra
                         cara, amorosa) it, e

1306 Vivaldi, Antonio   Someone, I know not who (Un certo
                         non so che) it, e

Taken altogether, these three volumes are excellent in
choice, difficulty and ranges.

FORTY FRENCH SONGS, VOL. I

Selected and edited by Sergius Kagen

International Music Co., 1952

Key and Range

Low   High

1307 Bachelet, Alfred   Chère nuit

1308 Berlioz, Hector   L'Absence

1309 Berlioz, Hector   Villanelle

1310 Chabrier, Emmanuel   Villanelle des petits canards

1311 Chabrier, Emmanuel   Les cigales

1312 Chabrier, Emmanuel   Ballade des gros dindons

1313 Dupont, Gabriel   Mandoline

1314 deFalla, Manuel   Seguidille

1315 Franck, César   La Procession

1316 Franck, César   Nocturne

1317 Georges, Alexandre   Hymne au soleil

Low   High

1318 Georges, Alexandre   La Pluie

1319 Gounod, Charles   Venise

1320 Koechlin, Charles   L'Hiver

1321 Koechlin, Charles   Si tu le veux

1322 Koechlin, Charles   Le Thé

1323 Liszt, Franz   Oh, guand je dors

1324 Paladilhe   Psyché

1325 Saint-Saens, Camille   Aimons-nous

1326 Saint-Saens, Camille   L'Attente

1327 Saint-Saens, Camille   Le Bonheur est chose légère

1328 Saint-Saens, Camille   Danse Macabre

Forty songs in two volumes, not forty in each. In this collection, one finds many songs and composers that are otherwise difficult to find. Each song is provided with an English translation. Certainly one of the better anthologies of French song to be found.

119

FORTY FRENCH SONGS, VOLUME II

Selected and edited by Sergius Kagen

International Music Co., 1952

Key and Range

		Low	High
1329	Bemberg, Henri	Il neige	
1330	Bizet, George	Ouvre ton coeur	
1331	Bizet, George	Chanson d'Avril	
1332	Bruneau, Alfred	Le sabot de frene	
1333	Bruneau, Alfred	L'Heureaux vagabond	
1334	Delibes, Leo	Les filles de Cadix	
1335	Ferrari, Gustave	Le Miroir	
1336	Flegier, Ange	Le Cor	
1337	Hahn, Reynaldo	L'Heure exquise	
1338	Hahn, Reynaldo	Offrande	
1339	Hahn, Reynaldo	Si mes vers avaient des ailes	

		Low	High
1340 Huë, Georges	Les clochettes des muguets		
1341 Huë, Georges	J'ai pleuré en rêve		
1342 Huë, Georges	A des oiseaux		
1343 d'Indy, Vincent	Lied maritime		
1344 d'Indy, Vincent	Madrigal		
1345 Liszt, Franz	Oh, quand je dors		
1346 Massenet, Jules	Crépuscule		
1347 Pierné, Gabriel	Le Moulin		
1348 Poldowski	Dansons la gigue		
1349 Poldowski	L'Heure exquise		
1350 Szulc, Joseph	Clair de lune		

See note page 119.

Ashley Publications, Inc., 1976

Key and Range

1351 Berlioz, Hector   Villanelle, fr, e

1352 Bizet, Georges   In the woods (Vieille chanson) fr, e

1353 Bizet, Georges   Pastoral (Pastorale)fr, e

1354 Blanc, Claudius   Perfume of a flower (Parfum de fleur)fr, e

1355 Bouval, Jules ·   A flower message (Fleur messagère) fr, e

1356 Bouval, Jules   The clouds (Les Nuages) fr, e

1357 Breville, Pierre de   The ferret (Le furet du bois joli) fr, e

1358 Chaminade, Cécile   If thou shouldst tell me (Tu me dirais)fr,e

1359 Chaminade, Cécile   Were I gardener (Si j'étais jardinier)fr,e

1360 Chausson, Ernest   The dead (Les morts) fr, e

1361 Chretien, Hedwige   Could I forget (Que je t'oublie) fr, e

1362 Cozuard, Arthur   Haï Luli, fr, e

1363 Debussy, Claude   The bells (Les cloches) fr, e

1364 Debussy, Claude   The death of lovers (La mort des amants)fr,e

1365 Debussy, Claude   Evening harmony (Harmonie du soir) fr, e

1366 Debussy, Claude   Romance, fr, e

1367 Debussy, Claude   The shadow of trees (L'ombre des arbres)fr,e

1368 Debussy, Claude   The tears fall in my soul (Il pleure dans mon coeur)fr, e

1369 Delibes, Leo   Bygone days (Jours passés) fr, e

1370 Delibes, Leo   The maids of Cadiz (Les filles de Cadix)fr,e

1371 Duparc, Henri   Ecstasy (Extase) fr, e

1372 Duparc, Henri   A sigh (Soupir)

1373 Fauré, Gabriel   Moonlight (Clair de lune)fr, e

1374 Fauré, Gabriel   The roses of Ispahan (Les roses d'Ispahan) fr, e

1375 Ferrari, G.   I've such a host of things to tell you (J'ai tant de choses à vous dire) fr, e

1376 Fontenailles, H. de   Winter roses (Roses d'hiver) fr, e

1377 Franck, Cesar   The gathered rose (Lied) fr, e

1378 Franck, Cesar   Marriage of roses (Le mariage des roses)fr,e

1379 Hahn, Reynaldo   Chanson d'automne, fr

1380 Hahn, Reynaldo   D'une prison, fr

A good collection and good value. All songs are translated but
there are occasional editing lapses.

ANTHOLOGY OF MODERN FRENCH SONG

Thirty-nine Songs

Collected and edited by Max Spicker

G. Schirmer, Inc., 1912, 1939

Key and   Range

Low   High

1381 Bachelet, Alfred   Dearest night (Chère nuit)fr, e

1382 Bizet, Georges   In the woods (Vieille Chanson)fr, e

1383 Bruneau, Alfred   The gay vagabond (L'Heureux vaga-
                             bond)fr, e

1384 Chausson, Ernest   Butterflies (Les papillons)fr, e

1385 Chausson, Ernest   The charm (Le charme)fr, e   SAME

1386 Coquard, Arthur   Sad and lonely (Haï-luli)fr, e

1387 Debussy, Claude   Evening fair (Beau soir)fr, e

1388 Debussy, Claude   Her hair (La chevelure)fr, e   SAME

1389 Debussy, Claude   Mandolin (Mandoline)fr, e

1390 Debussy, Claude   Romance, fr, e

1391 Delibes, Leo   Good-morning, Sue (Bonjour, Suzon)
                             fr, e   125

1392 D'Indy, Vincent	A sea song (Lied maritime)fr, e	
1393 Duparc, Henri	A song of sorrow (Chanson triste)fr,e	
1394 Duparc, Henri	Invitation to the journey (L'invitation au voyage)fr, e	
1395 Fauré, Gabriel	After a dream (Aprés un rêve)fr, e	
1396 Fauré, Gabriel	The cradles (Les berceaux)fr, e	
1397 Fauré, Gabriel	Evening (Soir)fr, e	
1398 Fauré, Gabriel	A meeting (Rencontre) fr, e	
1399 Fauré, Gabriel	Nell, fr, e	
1400 Fauré, Gabriel	The rose of Ispahan (Les roses d'Ispahan)fr, e	
1401 Franck, Cesar	The marriage of the roses (Le mariage des roses)fr, e	
1402 Hüe, Georges	Breezes of other days (Brises d'autrefois)fr, e	
1403 Lalo, Edouard	The bondmaid (L'esclave)fr, e	
1404 Lalo, Edouard	The lark's song (La chanson de l'Alouette)fr, e	
1405 Lekeu, Guillaume	On a tomb (Sur une tombe)fr, e	
1406 Leroux, Xavier	The Nile (Le Nil)fr, e	
1407 Massenet, Jules	The first dance (Première Danse)fr,e	

126

1408 Paladilhe, E.   Psyche, fr, e

1409 Paladilhe, E.   Three prayers (Les trois prières)fr,e

1410 Paladilhe, E.   The wren (Le roitelet)fr, e

1411 Pierné, G.   To Lucette (A Lucette)fr, e

1412 Saint-Saens, C.   The bell (La cloche)fr, e

1413 Saint-Saens, C.   Moonrise (Le lever de la lune)fr, e

1414 Saint-Saens, C.   In solitude (La solitaire)fr, e

1415 Vidal, Paul   The faithful heart (Le fidele coeur)
                            fr, e

1416 Vidal, Paul   Were I sunshine, I should come
                            (Ariette)fr, e

1417 Widor, Charles   Albaÿde, fr, e

1418 Widor, Charles   Nothing I ask thee to give me (Je ne
                            veux pas autre chose)fr, e

1419 Widor, Charles   Starry night (Nuit d'ètoiles)fr, e

This collection has been around quite awhile but is
still useful and worth having.

FRENCH DICTION SONGS

From the 17th to the 20th Centuries

Edited by Anne and William Leyerle

Leyerle Publications, 1983, Box 384, Geneseo, NY 14454

Key and Range

1420 Berlioz, Hector   L'Absence

1421 Bernstein, Leonard   Civet à toute Vitesse

1422 Bizet, Georges   La chanson du fou

1423 Chabrier, Emmanuel   Villanelle des petits canards

1424 Chausson, Ernest   Le charme

1425 Debussy, Claude   Les Angélus

1426 Debussy, Claude   Rondel (Le temps a laissié son Manteau)

1427 Duparc, Henri   Le Manoir de Rosamonde

1428 Fauré, Gabriel   En Sourdine

1429 Franck, Cesar   Lied

1430 Hahn, Reynaldo   D'une prison

128

1431 Johnston, Jack   La Chanson de la Glu

1432 Lully, J. B.   Je languis nuit et jour

1433 Mozart, W. A.   Dans un bois solitaire

1434 Paladilhe, Emile   Pastel

1435 Rameau, J. P.   Vous excitez la plus sincère ardeur

1436 Ravel, Maurice   Cinq mélodies populaire Grecques
                                    1. Le réveil de la mariée

                                    2. Là-bas, vers l'église

                                    3. Quel galant

                                    4. Chanson des cueilleuses de
                                        lentisques

                                    5. Tout gai!

1437 Rousseau, J. J.   L'amour croit s'il si'inquiète

1438 Saint-Saens, C.   Clair de lune

1439 Ward-Steinman, David   Les odes de jeunesse
                                    1. À la forêt de Gastine

                                    2. À la fontaine Bellerie

This is a new anthology, which I am sure will become widely
known and used. The choice of songs is excellent and most are
for medium voice. The phonetic transcription (in IPA symbols)
is provided immediately under the French text. A precise explanation of French sounds and IPA symbols is supplied and then follows
a commentary and word-for-word translation of each song. Finally,
the Greek text to Ravel's "Five Greek Songs" is provided along
with a phonetic transcription and English translation. All this
is put under the voice line.

In all, an impressive anthology.

FIFTY SELECTED SONGS BY

SCHUBERT, SCHUMANN, BRAHMS, WOLF AND STRAUSS

English texts by Florence Easton

G. Schirmer, Inc., 1951

Key and Range

Low   High

1440 Brahms, Johannes   Forest Solitude (In Waldesein-
                               samkeit) g,e

1441 Brahms, Johannes   In the churchyard (Auf dem
                               Kirchhofe) g,e

1442 Brahms, Johannes   The message (Botschaft) g,e

1443 Brahms, Johannes   My love is green (Meine Liebe
                               ist grün) g,e

1444 Brahms, Johannes   My thoughts like haunting music
                               (Wie Melodien zieht es mir) g,e

1445 Brahms, Johannes   O come, delightful summer night
                               (O komme, holde Sommernacht) g,e

1446 Brahms, Johannes   Of eternal love (Von ewiger
                               Liebe) g,e

1447 Brahms, Johannes   Oh, death is still and cool as
                               night (Der Tod, das ist die
                               kühle Nacht) g,e

1448 Brahms, Johannes   Serenade (Ständchen) g,e

1449 Brahms, Johannes   The vain suit (Vergebliches
                               Ständchen) g,e

1450 Schubert, Franz.   The butterfly (Der Schmetter-
                               ling) g,e
                               131

1451 Schubert, Franz	Evening violets (Nachtviolen) g,e	
1452 Schubert, Franz	Hedge-roses (Heidenröslein) g,e	
1453 Schubert, Franz	Impatience (Ungeduld) g,e	
1454 Schubert, Franz	In the red of evening (Im Abend-roth) g,e	
1455 Schubert, Franz	The lover's metamorphoses (Lieb-haber in allen Gestalten) g,e	
1456 Schubert, Franz	Night and dreams (Nacht und Träume) g,e	
1457 Schubert, Franz	Omnipotence (Die Allmacht) g,e	
1458 Schubert, Franz	Restless love (Rastlose Liebe) g,e	
1459 Schubert, Franz	Whither? (Wohin?) g,e	
1460 Schumann, Robert	By moonlight (Mondnacht) g,e	
1461 Schumann, Robert	Dedication (Widmung) g,e	
1462 Schumann, Robert	The lotus-flower (Die Lotosblume) g,e	
1463 Schumann, Robert	Messages (Aufträge) g,e	
1464 Schumann, Robert	My lovely star (Mein schöner Stern) g,e	
1465 Schumann, Robert	Snowbells (Schneeglöckchen) g,e	
1466 Schumann, Robert	Spring night (Frühlingsnacht) g,e	

1467 Schumann, Robert	The walnut tree (Der Nussbaum) g,e	
1468 Schumann, Robert	With myrtle and roses (Mit Myrthen und Rosen) g,e	
1469 Schumann, Robert	You are just like a flower (Du bist wie eine Blume) g,e	
1470 Strauss, Richard	All Souls' Day (Allerseelen) g,e	
1471 Strauss, Richard	Cecilia (Cäcilie) g,e	
1472 Strauss, Richard	Dedication (Zueignung) g,e	
1473 Strauss, Richard	Dream in the twilight (Traum durch die Dämmerung) g,e	
1474 Strauss, Richard	Homecoming (Heimkehr) g,e	
1475 Strauss, Richard	I wear my love (Ich trage meine Minne) g,e	
1476 Strauss, Richard	Rest now, weary spirit (Ruhe, meine Seele) g,e	
1477 Strauss, Richard	Secret invitation (Heimliche Aufforderung) g,e	
1478 Strauss, Richard	Serenade (Ständchen) g,e	
1479 Strauss, Richard	Tomorrow (Morgen) g,e	
1480 Wolf, Hugo	At daybreak (In der Frühe) g,e	
1481 Wolf, Hugo	Farewell (Lebe wohl) g,e	
1482 Wolf, Hugo	From her balcony green (Auf dem grünen Balcon) g,e	

133

1483 Wolf, Hugo	Go forth now, sweet Mary (Nun wandre, Maria) g,e	
1484 Wolf, Hugo	If you desire to see a dying lover (Und willst du deinen Liebsten sterben sehen) g,e	
1485 Wolf, Hugo	Insatiable love (Nimmersatte Liebe) g,e	
1486 Wolf, Hugo	In the shadow of my tresses (In dem Schatten meiner Locken) g,e	
1487 Wolf, Hugo	Mignon (kennst du das Land) g,e	
1488 Wolf, Hugo	Secrecy (Verborgenheit) g,e	
1489 Wolf, Hugo	The unpretentious love (Bescheidene Liebe) g,e	

57 CLASSIC PERIOD SONGS

Selected, translated, transposed and edited by

Van Christy and Carl Zytowski

Belwin-Mills Publishing Co., 1968

Key and Range

Med Low   Med High

1490 Bach, C. P. E.   Christmas song (Weihnachtslied)
                             g,e

1491 Bach, C. P. E.   Prayer (Bitten) g,e

1492 Beethoven, L. van   Adelaide (Adelaide) g,e

1493 Beethoven, L. van   The glory of God in nature (Die
                             Ehre Gottes in der Natur) g,e

1494 Beethoven, L. van   In yon dark tomb (In questa tomba
                             oscura) it,e

1495 Beethoven, L. van   I love you (Ich liebe dich) g,e

1496 Beethoven, L. van   Joyful and fearful, (Freudvoll und
                             leidvoll) g,e

1497 Beethoven, L. van   The kiss (Der Kuss) g,e

1498 Beethoven, L. van   Longing (Sehnsucht) g,e

1499 Beethoven, L. van   Mignon (Mignon) g,e

1500 Beethoven, L. vàn   New love, new life (Neue Liebe,
                             neues Leben) g,e

1501 Beethoven, L. van	The Parting (La Partenza) it,e
1502 Beethoven, L. van	A prayer (Bitten) g,e
1503 Beethoven, L. van	Song for Frau von Weissenthurn (Lied für Frau von Weissenthurn) g,e
1504 Beethoven, L. van	Song of May (Mailied) g,e
1505 Beethoven, L. van	Song of penitence (Busslied) g,e
1506 Beethoven, L. van	To the distant beloved (An die ferne Geliebte) g,e
1507 Gluck, C. W.	Summer night (Die Sommernacht) g,e
1508 Gretry, A. E. M.	Ballad (Couplets) fr,e
1509 Haydn, F. J.	Country joy (Die Landlust) g,e
1510 Haydn, F. J.	Despair e
1511 Haydn, F. J.	Equals (Der Gleichsinn) g,e
1512 Haydn, F. J.	In praise of laziness (Lob der Faulheit) g,e
1513 Haydn, F. J.	Life is a dream (Das Leben ist ein Traum) g,e
1514 Haydn, F. J.	My mother bids me bind my hair e
1515 Haydn, F. J.	Piercing eyes e
1516 Haydn, F. J.	She never told her love e

1517 Haydn, F. J.	A song of spring (Bald wehen uns des Frühlings Lufte) g,e	
1518 Haydn, F. J.	The spirit's song	
1519 Haydn, F. J.	A very commonplace story (Ein sehr gewöhnliche Geschichte) g,e	
1520 Haydn, F. J.	Virtue and beauty (Als einst mit Weibes Schönheit) g,e	
1521 Haydn, F. J.	The wanderer e	
1522 Hopkinson, Francis	Beneath a weeping willow's shade	
1523 Hopkinson, Francis	My days have been so wondrous free	
1524 Mozart, W. A.	Contentment (Die Zufriedenheit) g,e	
1525 Mozart, W. A.	Evening thoughts of Laura (Abend-empfindung) g,e	
1526 Mozart, W. A.	Farewell (Addio) it,e	
1527 Mozart, W. A.	Give me your promise (Vedrai, carino from "Don Giovanni") it,e	
1528 Mozart, W. A.	Great creator (Ave verum corpus) l,e	
1529 Mozart, W. A.	Journeyman's song (Lied zur Gesellenreise) g,e	
1530 Mozart, W. A.	Longing for spring (Sehnsucht nach dem Frühling) g,e	
1531 Mozart, W. A.	The old woman (Die Alte) g,e	
1532 Mozart, W. A.	The sorcerer (Der Zauberer) g,e	

1533 Mozart, W. A.	To Chloe (An Chloe) g,e	
1534 Mozart, W. A.	The violet (Das Veilchen) g,e	
1535 Mozart, W. A.	When Louise burned the letters from her untrue lover (Als Luise die Briefe ihres ungetreuen Liebhabers) g,e	
1536 Neefe, Christian	Eulogy (Das Totenopfer) g,e	
1537 Neefe, Christian	Serenade (Serenate) g,e	
1538 Reichardt, Johann	Courage (Mut) g,e	
1539 Reichardt, Johann	The lovely night (Die schöne Nacht) g,e	
1540 Sack, Johann	Ode g,e	
1541 Schubart, Christian	Christmas song of the shepherds (Weihnachtslied der Hirten) g,e	
1542 Unknown	Dearest maiden hear my song (Liebes Mädchen hor' mir zu g,e	
1543 Unknown	Lullaby (Wiegenlied) g,e	
1544 Zelter, Carl	None but the longing heart (Sehnsucht) g,e	
1545 Zelter, Carl	Restless love (Rastlose Liebe) g,e	
1546 Zumsteeg, Johann	The tree of love (Der Baum der Liebe) g,e	

In addition to being an excellent collection for any
level, it is also a good source for hard-to-find songs
of pre-Schubert composers.

GERMAN ART SONGS

FOR SCHOOL AND STUDIO

Edited by Bernard Taylor

Oliver Ditson, Co., 1947

Key and Range

Med Low   Med High

1547	Brahms, Johannes	The disappointed serenader (Vergebliches Ständchen)g, e	
1548	Brahms, Johannes	My heart is in bloom (Meine Liebe ist grün)g, e	
1549	Brahms, Johannes	Oh, Death is like the cooling night (Der Tod, das ist die kühle Nacht)g,e	
1550	Brahms, Johannes	O that I might retrace the way (O wüsst' ich doch den Weg zurück)g, e	
1551	Schubert, Franz	Death and the maiden (Der Tod und das Mädchen)g, e	
1552	Schubert, Franz	Restless love (Rastlose Liebe)g, e	
1553	Schubert, Franz	The Wanderer (Der Wanderer) g, e	
1554	Schubert, Franz	Whither? (Wohin?)g, e	
1555	Schumann, Robert	Dedication (Widmung)g, e	
1556	Schumann, Robert	I'll not complain (Ich grolle nicht) g, e	
1557	Schumann, Robert	Moonlight (Mondnacht)g, e	

139

1558 Schumann, Robert   'Tis spring (Er ist's)g, e

1559 Wolf, Hugo   Secrecy (Verborgenheit)g, e

1560 Wolf, Hugo   Song to spring (Er ist's)g, e

1561 Wolf, Hugo   To rest, to rest (Zur Ruh, zur Ruh)
                                g, e

1562 Wolf, Hugo   Tramping (Fussreise) g, e

A good basic collection, with some songs not contained
in other anthologies. Does contain a section on German
pronunciation.

140

SONGS BY TWENTY TWO AMERICANS

Compiled by Bernard Taylor

G. Schirmer, Inc., 1960

Range

Low   High

1563 Barber, Samuel	Sure on this shining night	
1564 Bernstein, Leonard	Plum pudding	
1565 Bowles, Paul	Once a lady was here	
1566 Carpenter, J. A.	Serenade	
1567 Charles, Ernest	O lovely world	
1568 Charles, Ernest	The Sussex sailor	
1569 Creston, Paul	The bird of the wilderness	
1570 Dougherty, Celius	Love in the dictionary	
1571 Dougherty, Celius	Primavera	
1572 Duke, John	A piper	
1573 Duke, John	Loveliest of trees	

141

1574	Edwards, Clara	Into the night	
1575	Edwards, Clara	Ol' Jim	
1576	Griffes, Charles	By a lonely forest pathway (Auf geheimem Waldespfade) g,e	
1577	Griffes, Charles	The lament of Ian the Proud	
1578	Hageman, Richard	Do not go, my love	
1579	McArthur, Edwin	Night	
1580	Malotte, Albert Hay	Upstream	
1581	Naginski, Charles	The pasture	
1582	Rich, Gladys	American lullaby	
1583	Roy, William	This little rose	
1584	Sacco, John	That's life	
1585	Sargent, Paul	Manhattan joy ride	
1586	Thomson, Virgil	Preciosilla	
1587	Tyson, Mildred Lund	Sea moods	
1588	Warren, Elinor Remick	Snow toward evening	
1589	Wolfe, Jacques	De glory road	

A NEW ANTHOLOGY OF AMERICAN SONG

25 Songs by Native American Composers

G. Schirmer, Inc., 1958

		<u>Low out of Print</u>	Key and Range High
1590 Barber, Samuel	The Daisies		
1591 Beach, Mrs. H. H. A.	Meadow-larks		
1592 Cadman, Charles W.	A moonlight song		
1593 Campbell-Tipton, Louis	The Crying of water (Le Cri des Eaux) fr,e		
1594 Carpenter, J. A.	Looking-glass river		
1595 Charles, Ernest	And so, Goodbye		
1596 Crist, Bainbridge	Knock on the door		
1597 Deis, Carl	A lover's lament		
1598 Farwell, Arthur	On a faded violet		
1599 Griffes, Charles	The Lament of Ian the Proud		
1600 Guion, David	Mary alone		

143

1601 Hadley, Henry	The rose-leaves are falling like rain (Il pleut des pétales de fleurs) fr,e	
1602 Homer, Sidney	Down Bye street	
1603 Horsman, Edward	The Bird of the wilderness	
1604 Kingsford, Charles	Wall-paper	
1605 Kramer, A. Walter	I have seen dawn	
1606 LaForge, Frank	Retreat (Schlupfwinkel) g,e	
1607 Malotte, Albert Hay	The Homing heart	
1608 Manning, Kathleen L.	Shoes	
1609 Powell, John	Heartsease	
1610 Spalding, Albert	The Rock of rubies	
1611 Still, Wm. Grant	The Breath of a rose	
1612 Stillman-Kelley, Edgar	Eldorado	
1613 Watts, Wintter	Wings of night	
1614 Woodman, R. Huntington	I am thy harp	

20th CENTURY ART SONGS

Medium Voice

G. Schirmer, Inc., 1967

Key and Range

1615 Barber, Samuel   Under the willow tree (from "Vanessa")

1616 Bernstein, Leonard   It must be me (from "Candide")

1617 Bliss, Arthur   The Buckle

1618 Bowles, Paul   Cabin

1619 Creston, Paul   Psalm XXIII

1620 Dougherty, Celius   Across the Western Ocean

1621 Dougherty, Celius   The k'e

1622 Dougherty, Celius   A minor bird

1623 Dougherty, Celius   Thy fingers make early flowers

1624 Duke, John   I watched the Lady Caroline

1625 Duke, John   Silver

145

1626 Gibbs, C. Armstrong	To one who passed whistling through the night	
1627 Gold, Ernest	Music, when soft voices die	
1628 Gold, Ernest	Parting	
1629 Griffes, Charles T.	Symphony in yellow	
1630 Guion, David	At the cry of the first bird	
1631 Kingsley, Herbert	The green dog	
1632 Menotti, Gian Carlo	The black swan (from "The Medium")	
1633 Menotti, Gian Carlo	The hero	
1634 Roberton, Hugh	All in the April evening	
1635 Sacco, John	Brother Will, brother John	
1636 Schirmer, Rudolf	Honey Shun	
1637 Schuman, William	Orpheus with his lute	
1638 Shaw, Martin	Song of the palanquin bearers	
1639 Thomson, Virgil	My crow Pluto	
1640 Weaver, Powell	Moon-marketing	
1641 Weill, Kurt	The lonesome dove (from "Down in the Valley")	

This is an outstanding song collection with several advantages: all songs are in English, and many of our better-known and more prolific song composers are represented. Most are difficult and some are for voices higher than medium. An advanced student would gain much from this collection.

CONTEMPORARY ART SONGS

28 Songs by American and British Composers

G. Schirmer, Inc., 1970

Range

1642 Barber, Samuel   Must the winter come so soon? (From "Vanessa")

1643 Beck, John Ness   Song of devotion

1644 Bernstein, Leonard   Two love songs: Extinguish my eyes

When my soul touches yours

1645 Bowles, Paul   Heavenly grass

1646 Carpenter, J. A.   When I bring to you colour'd toys

1647 Chávez, Carlos   The reaper (Segador) sp,e

1648 Chenoweth, Wilbur   Vocalise

1649 Corigliano, John   Christmas at the cloisters

1650 Corigliano, John   The unicorn

1651 Dougherty, Celius   Sound the flute!

1653	Duke, John	Peggy Mitchell
1654	Dunhill, Thomas	To the queen of heaven
1655	Gibbs, C. Armstrong	When I was one-and-twenty
1656	Hoiby, Lee	An immorality
1657	Kingsford, Charles	Down Harly street
1658	Menotti, Gian Carlo	Lullaby (from "The Consul")
1659	Moore, Douglas	The dove song (from "The Wings of the Dove")
1660	Sargent, Paul	Stopping by woods on a snowy evening
1661	Schuman, William	Holiday song
1662	Shaw, Martin	Easter carol
1663	Symons, Dom Thomas	A sight in camp
1664	Thiman, Eric H.	I love all graceful things
1665	Thomson, Virgil	English Usage
1666	Thomson, Virgil	The tiger
1667	Toye, Francis	The inn
1668	Vaughan Williams, R.	Hugh's song of the road

1669 Wells, Howard   Everyone sang

SONGS IN ENGLISH

Eighteen Contemporary Settings

by American and English Composers

Edited by Bernard Taylor

Carl Fischer, Inc., 1970

Range

Med Low   Med High

1670 Duke, John   Be still as you are beautiful

1671 Duke, John   Evening

1672 Duke, John   Just-spring

1673 Duke, John   Spring thunder

1674 Dello Joio, Norman   How do I love thee?

1675 Dello Joio, Norman   Why so pale and wan, fond lover?

1676 Dougherty, Celius   Heaven-haven

1677 Dougherty, Celius   The taxi

1678 Elgar, Edward   Pleading

1679 Elgar, Edward   Sabbath morning at sea

1680 Elgar, Edward   Sea slumber song

151

1681 Elgar, Edward   Where corals lie

1682 Holst, Gustav   Vedic Hymns: Ushas (Dawn)

1683 Holst, Gustav   Varuna I (Sky)

1684 Holst, Gustav   Varuna II (The waters)

1685 McArthur, Edwin   Spring day

1686 Morgenstern, Sam   My apple tree

1687 Nordoff, Paul   Song of innocence

Another good collection, well-chosen but not too
difficult. Also includes notes on composers and
authors, as well as hints on singing English.

CONTEMPORARY SONGS IN ENGLISH

Edited by Bernard Taylor

Carl Fischer, Inc., 1956

Range

Med Low   Med High

1688 Bergsma, William   Lullee, lullay

1689 Bone, Gene and Fenton,   Deborah
         Howard

1690 Cooper, Esther   Enough

1691 Dello Joio, Norman   Mill doors

1692 Dello Joio, Norman   There is a lady sweet and kind

1693 Duke, John   Bells in the rain

1694 Duke, John   Luke Havergal

1695 Edmunds, John   The lonely

1696 Freed, Isadore   Chartless

1697 Harris, Roy   Fog

1698 Helm, Everett   Prairie waters by night

153

1699 Holst, Gustav   Indra

1700 Howe, Mary   Let us walk in the white snow

1701 Moore, Douglas   Old song

1702 Moore, Douglas   Under the greenwood tree

1703 Vaughan Williams, R.   Silent noon

A good collection of songs by 20th century composers, strong in musical worth but not too difficult for most intermediate students.

CONTEMPORARY AMERICAN SONGS

Compiled and Edited by Bernard Taylor

Summy-Birchard Publishing Co., 1960

Reprinted with permission by Frangipani Press

Low   High

1704 Beach, Bennie   Peace

1705 Bialosky, Marshall   An old picture

1706 Branscombe, Gena   Old woman rain

1707 Donato, Anthony   To my neighbor at the concert

1708 Kalmanoff, Martin   Twentieth century

1709 Kettering, Eunice   Compensation

1710 Kreutz, Robert   December lark

1711 Latham, William   The new love and the old

1712 Lekberg, Sven   Birds singing at dusk

1713 Murray, Bain   The pasture

1714 Pfautsch, Lloyd   Lute book lullaby

155

1715 Raphling, Sam   Fugue on "money"

1716 Read, Gardiner   A white blossom

1717 Work, John W.   Three glimpses of night

An excellent collection for an intermediate level student.
The songs are not too difficult yet provide variety of
musical experience and of text. Well worth having.

AMERICAN ART-SONG ANTHOLOGY
High voice and piano
Volume 1, Edited by John Belisle
Galaxy Music Corporation, 1982

Range

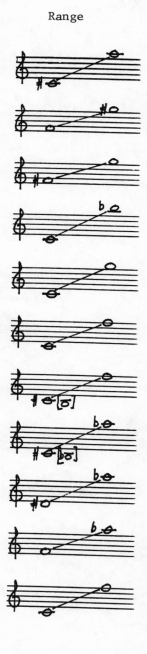

1718 Beeson, Jack   Eldorado

1719 Benshoof, Kenneth   The cow

1720 Benshoof, Kenneth   The fox

1721 Berg, Christopher   Last letter

1722 Childs, Barney   Virtue

1723 Cumming, Richard   Other loves
                                  1)   Summer Song

1724 Cumming, Richard   2)   Night Song

1725 Cumming, Richard   3)   Love Song

1726 Gideon, Miriam   Gone in good sooth you are

1727 Green, Ray   I loved my friend

1728 Ivey, Jean E.   I would live in your love

1729 Ivey, Jean E.	To one away
1730 Lindenfeld, Harris	Dolor
1731 Lindenfeld, Harris	The cow
1732 Rorem, Ned	The youth with the red-gold hair
1733 Ward-Steinman, David	Season
1734 Wood, Kevin	Ants will not eat your fingers 1) Girl's song
1735 Wood, Kevin	2) Second song
1736 Wood, Kevin	3) Ants will not eat your fingers
1737 Zaimont, Judith L.	Soliloquy

This collection is not for the faint-hearted or the musically
insecure. Most songs were written after 1970 and are complicated
in meter, rhythms, vocal lines and accompaniments (including one
accompaniment for prepared piano). If one is looking for unusual
material for a musically sophisticated student, this might be the
collection.

CHAPTER III

BIBLIOGRAPHY OF IMPORTANT BOOKS

A. Voice Production

Appelman, D. Ralph. The Science of Vocal Pedagogy. Bloomington: University
    of Indiana Press, 1967.

Bachner, Louis. Dynamic Singing. New York: A. A. Wyn, Inc., 1944.

Brown, William Earl. Vocal Wisdom: Maxims of Giovanni Battista Lamperti.
    Enlarged edition with supplement by Lillian Strongin. New York:
    Arno Press, Inc., 1957.

Burgin, John Carroll. Teaching Singing. Metuchen, N. J.: Scarecrow Press,
    1973.
        This is a valuable and very useful book, a continuation of Victor
    Fields's Training the Singing Voice.

Christy, Van C. Expressive Singing, Basic Textbook. Dubuque, Iowa: Wm. C.
    Brown Co., 1967.

--------. Expressive Singing, Volume 2. (Pedagogy, production theory and
    technic, style and interpretation, song repertoire, principles of
    piano accompaniment, solo voice and accompaniment recordings.) Dubuque,
    Iowa: Wm. C. Brown Co., 1975.

Coffin, Berton. Coffin's Overtones of Bel Canto. Phonetic Basis of Artistic
    Singing with 100 Chromatic Vowel-Chart Exercises. Metuchen, N. J.:
    Scarecrow Press, 1980.

--------. The Sounds of Singing: Vocal Techniques With Vowel-Pitch Charts.
    Metuchen, N. J.: Scarecrow Press, 1976.
        In many ways this is a useful book. In addition to Dr. Coffin's
    ideas on, and use of, resonance charts and the echophone, there is a
    section of over 20 pages of maxims of Paola Novikova, readings on
    register and breathing techniques, Pierre Delattre's article "The
    Radiography of vowels and its acoustic Correlations", and a wonderful
    bibliography.

Fields, Victor. The Singer's Glossary. 450 Vocal Terms Defined. Boston:
    Boston Music Co., 1952.

--------. Training the Singing Voice. New York: King's Crown Press, 1947.

Frisell, Anthony. The Tenor Voice. Somerville, Mass.: Bruce Humphries Publishers, 1964.

———. The Baritone Voice. Boston: Crescendo Publishing Co., 1972.

Garcia, Manuel. A Complete Treatise on the Art of Singing, Part II. Collated, edited and translated by Donald Paschke, NY: Da Capo Press, 1975.

Husler, Frederick and Rodd-Marling, Yvonne. Singing; The Physical Nature of the Vocal Organ, Revised Edition. London: Hutchinson and Co., 1976.

Lamperti, Francesco. A Treatise on the Art of Singing. Revised and translated by J. L. Griffith. New York: G. Schirmer, Inc., 1980.

Mancini, Giambattista. Practical Reflections on Figured Singing. Compared, translated and edited by Edward Foreman. Champagne, Illinois: Pro Musica Press, 1967.

Manen, Lucie. The Art of Singing. London: Faber Music Ltd., 1974. Includes cassette recording.

Marchesi, Mathilde. Theoretical and Practical Method. New York: Dover Publications, 1970.

Miller, Richard. English, French, German and Italian Techniques of Singing: A Study in National Tonal Preferences and How They Relate to Functional Efficiency. Metuchen, N. J.: Scarecrow Press, 1977.

Monahan, Brent Jeffrey. The Art of Singing: A Compendium of Thoughts on Singing between 1777 and 1927. Metuchen, N. J.: Scarecrow Press, 1978. A companion work to Fields and Burgin.

Nielsen, Gerda. A New Guide to Good Singing. Ontario: The Avondale Press, 1975.

Rosewall, Richard B. Handbook of Singing. A Guide to Vocal Development for the Beginning Student and the Teacher-in-Training. Evanston, Ill: Summy-Birchard Co., 1961.

Vennard, William. Developing Voices. New York: Carl Fischer, Inc., 1973. (See review in NATS Bulletin 30, No. 3 [Feb/March 1974]:40.)

Vennard, William. Singing: The Mechanism and the Technic. Revised Edition. New York: Carl Fischer, Inc., 1967.

Whitlock, Weldon. Profiles in Vocal Pedagogy. Ann Arbor: Clifton Press, 1975. (See Review in NATS Bulletin 33, #3 [May 1977]:43.)

B. Song Lists

Berry, Corre. Vocal Chamber Duets: An Annotated Bibliography. New York: NATS Publications, 1981.

Boytim, Joan Frey. Solo Vocal Repertoire for Young Singers: An Annotated Bibliography. New York: NATS Publications, 1980. (250 W. 57th St., NY 10019)

Carman, Gaeddert, Myers and Resch. Art-Song in the United States: An Annotated Bibliography. New York: NATS Publications, 1976, supplement 1978.

Christy, Van. Expressive Singing, Textbook Volume II. Dubuque, Iowa: Wm. C. Brown, Co., 1975.
      Dr. Christy presents several different published lists including several that are graded and arranged by voice for use in high school solo contests. Also included are sections on Sacred Songs, Songs for Special Occasions, and Duets.

Coffin, Berton. Singer's Repertoire, 2nd edition. Metuchen, N.J.: Scarecrow Press, 1960.
      Separate volumes (or collected in one) for soprano, mezzo and alto, tenor, and baritone and bass. Each volume has a number of different categories, such as "Recital Openers," "Recital Closers," "Songs Employing Agility," and so on. An important, and very useful, book.

deCharms, Desiree and Breed, P. F. Songs in Collections. Detroit: Information Service, 1966.
      Comprehensive in scope and information, helpful in locating certain songs, composers, or poets. Ranges not given.

Emmons, Shirlee and Sonntag, Stanley. The Art of the Song Recital. New York: Schirmer Books, 1979.
      The repertoire lists in this very useful book are extensive. Categories include "Voice with Instruments," "Anthologies of Vocal Compositions with Instrumental Accompaniment," "Voice with other Voices," "Song Cycles, Sets and Collections," "Anthologies" and several others.

Espina, Noni. Repertoire for the solo voice. 2 volumes. Metuchen, N. J.: Scarecrow Press, 1977.
      This is a comprehensive guide to solo repertoire, covering nearly 10,000 songs and arias.

-------. Vocal Solos for Protestant Services, second edition, New York:
    Vita d'Arte, 1974.
        A very valuable and useful book for church musicians and teachers.
    The main part is a list of solos arranged by composer. Indices include
    Occasions, Voice Types, Titles, and Composers. I have used this book
    many times.

Grubb, Thomas. Singing in French: A Manual of French Diction and French
    Vocal Repertoire. New York: Schirmer Books, 1979.
        In addition to being one of the best books on French diction, it
    also contains a nearly comprehensive list of repertoire with publishers.
    One list is devoted to art-song, another to arias arranged by voice type.

Kagen, Sergius. Music for the Voice. Bloomington: University of Indiana
    Press, 1968.
        Still a very valuable and useful book. Sections include "Songs
    and airs before the 19th century", "Songs of the 19th and 20th centuries",
    "Folk songs", and "Operatic Excerpts".

Koopman, John. Selected Sacred Solos in Modern Idiom. Minneapolis: Augsburg
    Publishing House, 1965.
        A slim volume, useful though in providing music for church services.
    All necessary information is provided, including the first line of each
    text.

Leigh, Robert. Index to Song Books. New York: Da Capo Press, 1973.
        A title index to over 11,000 copies of almost 6,800 songs in 111
    song books published between 1933 and 1962.

Martin, Walter. Recommended Sacred Solos for the University-Level Student.
    New York: NATS Publications, 1978.

Trusler, Ivan and Ehret, Walter. Functional Lessons in Singing, second edition.
        In the back of this class-voice book is a list of songs, selected,
    graded and categorized. Lists are given for each voice type, and
    publishers are included.

The American Academy of Teachers of Singing offers a number of song lists, the
    complete set costing only $3.00. They are as follows:
    Song lists 1, 2 and 3 are now combined: Three hundred songs by American
        composers.
    Song List 4: One hundred sacred songs.
    Song List 5: One hundred songs by modern English composers.
    Song List 6: One hundred songs by modern British composers.
    Song List 7: Collections of arrangements of folksongs of Great Britain
        and America in English.
    Song List 8: Translations of Classic and Semi-Classic Songs.
    Song List 9: Songs for the first two years of study (in 3 parts).
    Song List 10: Recital songs by American composers.
    Song List 11: Sacred songs (with annotations).
    Song List 12: Contemporary American and British composers, with annota-
        tions (a 12 page list, 304 songs).
    For any or all of the above lists, write Earl Rogers, 920 Riverside Dr.,
        New York, 10032.

C. Pronunciation

Adler, Kurt. _Phonetic Diction in Singing_ (taken from his book _The Art of Accompanying and Coaching_). Minneapolis: University of Minnesota Press, 1965.

Brown, Sarle. _Super-Pronunciation in Singing; A Practical Approach to the Study of Voice_. Dallas: Crescendo Publications, Inc., 1977.

Coffin, Berton and Ralph Errolle, Warner Singer and Pierre Delattre. _Phonetic Readings of Songs and Arias_. Boulder: Pruett Press, Inc. 1964. Now available from Scarecrow Press, Metuchen, New Jersey.

Colorni, Evelina. _Singer's Italian_. New York: Schirmer Books, 1970.

Cox, Richard. _The Singer's Manual of French and German Diction_. New York: Schirmer Books, 1971.

Errolle, Ralph. _Italian Diction for Singers_. Boulder: Pruett Press, 1963.

Grubb, Thomas. _Singing in French: A Manual of French Diction and French Vocal Repertoire_. New York: Schirmer Books, 1979.
    This book has replaced all others and is the finest now available.

Halliday, John R. _Diction for Singers_. Revised Edition. Provo, Utah: Brigham Young University Press, 1970.

Jones, Archie, M. Irving Smith and Robert Walls. _Pronouncing Guide to French, German, Italian and Spanish_. New York: Carl Fischer, Inc., 1945.

Marshall, Madeleine. _The Singer's Manual of English Diction_. New York: G. Schirmer, Inc., 1946.

Moriarty, John. _Diction: Italian, Latin, French, German. The Sounds and 81 Exercises for Singing Them_. 2 volumes. Boston: E. C. Schirmer Music Col, 1975. (See review NATS Bulletin, 32, no. 1 [Oct. 1975]:38.)

Odom, William. _German for Singers: A Textbook of Diction and Phonetics_. New York: Schirmer Books, 1981. (For Review, see NATS Bulletin, 39, no. 1 [Sept/Oct 1982]:43.)
    This book has quickly become one of the best on the subject. It is well-organized, comprehensive, and has the added advantage of tapes available from the author.

Pfautsch, Lloyd. _English Diction for the Singer_. New York: Lawson-Gould Music Publishing Inc., 1971.

Rothmueller, M. *Pronunciation of German and German Diction*. Bloomington: Indiana University Printing Plant, 1978. Order by writing Indiana Music Center, P. O. Box 582, Bloomington, IN 47401. (See review in NATS Bulletin, 35, no. 3 [Jan/Feb 1979]:35.)

Scheil, Richard F. *A Manual of Foreign Language Dictions*. Fredonia, New York: Paladian Co., 1975. (P. O. Box 63, Zip Code 14063.) (See review in NATS Bulletin 33, no. 3 [Feb 1977]:41.)

Siebs, Theodore. *Deutsche Hochsprache*, Ed. Helmut de Boor and Paul Diels. Berlin: Gruyter & Co., 1956.

Uris, Dorothy. *To Sing in English*. New York: Boosey and Hawkes, 1971.

Wierenga, Leanne. *French Diction for the Singer* (A Phonetics Workbook). New York: Kenyon Publications, 1977. (For review, see NATS Bulletin, 35, no. 1 [Sept/Oct 1978]:31.)

Yersin, Marie and Jeanne. *The Yersin Phono-Rhythmic Method of French Pronunciation, Accent and Diction*. Philadelphia: J. B. Lippincott Co., 1924.
      Although long out of print, this little volume is quite valuable if one can be found.

D. Translations

Bernac, Pierre. _Francis Poulenc. The Man and his Songs._ Translated by
    Winifred Radford. New York: W. W. Norton and Col, Inc., 1977.

———. _The Interpretation of French Song._ Translations of song texts by
    Winifred Radford. New York: Praeger Publishers, 1970.

Brody, E. and Fowkes, R. T. _The German Lied and its Poetry._ New York:
    New York University Press, 1971.

Cobb, Margaret G. _The Poetic Debussy. A Collection of his song texts and
    Selected Letters._ Boston: Northeastern University Press, 1982.

Coffin, Singer and Delattre. _Word by Word Translations of Songs and Arias,_
    part I, German and French. Metuchen, New Jersey: Scarecrow Press,
    1966.

Fischer-Dieskau, Dietrich. _The Fischer-Dieskau Book of Lieder._ Translated
    by George Bird and Richard Stokes. New York: Alfred Knopf, 1977.

Meister, Barbara. _Nineteenth-Century French Song. Fauré, Chausson, Duparc,
    & Debussy._ Bloomington: Indiana University Press, 1980.
        Every song by the above named composers is translated and
    discussed. In addition, background and biographical material is given.

Miller, Phillip. _The Ring of Words: An Anthology of Song Texts._ New York:
    W. W. Norton.

Paquin, Marie-Therese. _Dix Cycles de (Ten Cycles of) Lieder. Beethoven,
    Brahms, Mahler, Schubert, Schumann._ Montreal: Les Presses de
    L'Universite de Montreal, 1977. (See Review in NATS Bulletin, 37,
    no. 1 [Sept/Oct 1980]:37.

Phillips, Lois. _Lieder line by line and word for word._ New York: Charles
    Scribner's Sons, 1979. (See Review in NATS Bulletin, 38, no.3
    [Jan/Feb 1982]:46.)

Prawer, S. S. _Penguin Book of Lieder._ Baltimore: Penguin Books, 1964.

Sams, Eric. _The Songs of Robert Schumann._ New York: W. W. Norton, 1969.

———. _The Songs of Hugo Wolf._ London: Oxford University Press, 1962.

Schoep, Arthur and Daniel Harris. _Word by Word Translations of Songs and
    Arias,_ part II, Italian. Metuchen, New Jersey: Scarecrow Press, 1972.

Schoep, Dunn, Greenwell and Kirchberger. _English Singing Translations of Foreign Language Art Songs._ New York: NATS Publications, 1976.

Stein, Jack. _Poem and Music in the German Lied from Gluck to Hugo Wolf._ Cambridge: Harvard University Press, 1971.

E.   Interpretation

Barford, Philip. _Mahler Symphonies and Songs_. Seattle: University of Washington, 1972. One of B. B. C. Music Guides.

Bernac, Pierre. _Francis Poulenc: The Man and his Songs_. Translated by Winifred Radford. New York: W. W. Norton and Co., Inc., 1977.

-------. _The Interpretation of French Song_. New York: Praeger Publishers, 1970.

Brody, E. and Fowkes, R. T. _The German Lied and its Poetry_. New York: New York University Press, 1971.

Brown, Maurice J. E. _Schubert Songs_. Seattle University of Washington, 1969. B. B. C. Music Guide.

Capell, Richard. _Schubert's Songs_. First published in 1928, it is now available in paperback. London: Pan Books Ltd., 1973.

Cobb, Margaret G. _The Poetic Debussy: A Collection of His Song Texts and Selected Letters_. Boston: Northeastern University Press, 1982.

Cottrell, Alan P. _Wilhelm Müller's Lyrical Song-Cycles: Interpretations and Texts_. Chapel Hill: The University of North Carolina Press, 1970.

Desmond, Astra. _Schumann Songs_. Seattle: University of Washington Press, 1972. B. B. C. Music Guide.

Friedberg, Ruth C. _America Comes of Age_. Volume I of 3-volume series: _American Art-Song and American Poetry_. Metuchen, New Jersey: The Scarecrow Press, 1981. (For review, see NATS Bulletin, 38, no.4 [March/April 1982] :37.)

Goldovsky, Boris, and Schoep, Arthur. _Bringing Soprano Arias to Life_. New York: G. Schirmer, 1973.

Greene, Harry Plunket. _Interpretation in Song_. London and New York: Macmillan and Co., 1924. (Reprinted by DaCapo Press, 1979.)

Harrison, Max. _The Lieder of Brahms_. New York: Praeger Publishers, 1972.

Jefferson, Alan. _The Lieder of Richard Strauss_. New York: Praeger Publishers, 1971.

Landau, Anneliese. _The Lied: The Unfolding of its Style_. Washington: University Press of America, 1980.

Lehmann, Lotte. *Eighteen Song Cycles*. *Studies in Their Interpretation*. New York: Praeger Publishers, 1972.

-------. *More than Singing*. *The Interpretation of Songs*. New York: Boosey and Hawkes, Inc., 1945.

Meister, Barbara. *An Introduction to the Art Song*: *A Guide to Listening Pleasure*. New York: Taplinger Publishing Co., 1980. (see review in NATS Bulletin 37, no. 1 [Sept/Oct 1980]:38-39.)

-------, *Nineteenth-Century French Song*: *Fauré*, *Chausson*, *Duparc* and *Debussy*. Bloomington, Indiana: Indiana University Press, 1980. (For review, see NATS Bulletin 37, no. 3 [Jan/Feb 1981]:42.)

Moore, Gerald. *Am I too Loud?* New York: Macmillan and Co., 1962.

-------. *Poet's Love: The Songs and Cycles of Schumann*. New York: Taplinger Publishing Co., 1981.

-------. *The Schubert Song Cycles*. London: Hamish Hamilton, 1975.

-------. *Singer and Accompanist*. New York: Macmillan and Co., 1954.

Northcote, Sydney. *Byrd to Britten*. *A Survey of English Song*. New York: Roy Publishing Inc., 1966.

Noske, Fritz. *French Song from Berlioz to Duparc*. Translated by Rita Benton. Revised edition, New York: Dover Publications, Inc., 1970. Extensive bibliography and list of songs.

Osborne, Charles. *The Concert Song Companion*: A guide to the classical repertoire. London: Gollancz, 1974.

Panzera, Charles. *Fifty French Songs*. Fifty Lessons in Style and Interpretation. New York: C. F. Peters, 1964.

Petersen, Barbara. *Ton und Wort: The Lieder of Richard Strauss*. Ann Arbor: UMI Research Press, 1980. (Review NATS, 37, no. 4 [Mar/Apr 1981]:50.)

Sams, Eric. *Brahms Songs*. Seattle: University of Washington, 1972. B.B.C. Music Guide.

-------, *The Songs of Robert Schumann*. New York: W. W. Norton, 1969.

-------, *The Songs of Hugo Wolf*. London: Oxford University Press, 1962.

Schiøtz, Aksel. *The Singer and his Art*. New York: Harper and Row, Publishers, 1970.

Spink, Ian. *English Song Dowland To Purcell*. New York: Charles Scribner's Sons, 1974. Excellent bibliography.

Stein, Jack. *Poem and Music in the German Lied from Gluck to Hugo Wolf*. Cambridge: Harvard University Press, 1971.

Stevens, Denis, ed. A History of Song. London: Hutchinson and Co., Ltd.,
    1960. Revised Edition, New York: W. W. Norton and Co., Inc., 1970.
    Available in paperback.

Upton, William Trent. Art-Song in America: A Study in the Development of
    American Music. Boston: Oliver Ditson Co., 1930.

Walsh, Stephen. The Lieder of Schumann. New York: Praeger Publishers, 1971.

Yerbury, Grace D. Song in America from Early Times to about 1850. Metuchen:
    The Scarecrow Press, 1971.

F. History of Singers, Singing and Style

1. Books

Bacilly, Bénigne de. A Commentary Upon The Art of Proper Singing.
    Translated and edited by Austin B. Caswell. New York: The Institute
    of Medieval Music, Ltd., 1968.

Brown, William Earl. Lamperti's Vocal Wisdom. New York: Arno Press Inc.,
    1957.

Caccini, Giulio. Le Nuove Musiche. Edited by H. Wiley Hitchcock. Madison:
    A-R Editions, Inc., 1970.
        Important not only for Hitchcock's introduction and text transla-
    tions, but also for Caccini's introduction in which he gives detailed
    descriptions of style and ornamentation. Includes all the music in
    modern notation.

Duey, Philip A. Bel Canto in its Golden Age. New York: King's Crown Press,
    1951.

Garcia, Manuel. A Complete Treatise on the Art of Singing, Part II. Tr.
    Donald Paschke. New York: CaCapo Press, 1975.

--------. Hints on Singing. London: Chappell (H. Klein revision, 1911).

Henderson, W. J. Early History of Singing. New York: AMS Press, Inc., 1969.
    (Reprint of 1921 edition.)

Heriot, Angus. The Castrati in Opera. London: Martin Secker and Warburg
    Ltd., 1956. Paperback edition DaCapo Press, New York, 1975. With
    Bibliography.

Kay, Elster. Bel Canto. Lond: Dennis Dobson, 1963.

Marchesi, Mathilde. Marchesi and Music. Passages from the Life of a Famous
    Singing Teacher. New York and London: 1898. Reprinted by DaCapo. 1978.

Pahlen, K. Great Singers: From the Seventeenth Century to the Present Day.
    New York: Stein and Day, 1974.

Pleasants, Henry. The Great Singers. New York: Simon and Schuster, 1966.
    With Bibliography.

Reid, Cornelius. Bel Canto, Principles and Practices. New York: Coleman-
    Ross Co., Inc., 1950.

Tosi, Francesco. _Observations on the Florid Song_. London: J. Wilcox, 1723. Available in reprint edition.

Ulrich, Bernhard. _Concerning the Principles of Voice Training During the A Cappella Period and Until the Beginning of Opera_ (1474-1640). Translated by John Seale, edited by Edward Foreman. Minneapolis: Pro Musica Press, N D. (P O Box 8523, Zip Code 55408.) (See Review in NATS Bulletin 30, no. 4 [May/June 1974]:37.)

2. Articles

Cyr, M. "Eighteenth-Century French and Italian Singing: Rameau's Writing for the Voice," _Music and Letters_, 61, no. 3-4 (1980):318.

Manen, Lucie. "Vocal Timbres, the Essence of the Classical School of Singing," _Studies in Music_, 13 (1979):34-43.

von Ramm, A. "Style in Early Music Singing," _Early Music_ 8, no. 1 (1980:17-20.

Sanford, S. A. "Seventeenth & Eighteenth Century Vocal Style & Technique," _Dissertation Abstracts_, 40 (Jan 1980):3621 A.

Uberti, M. "Vocal Techniques in Italy in the Second Half of the Sixteenth Century," _Early Music_, 9, no. 4 (1981):486-95.

Wadsworth, S. "Heavy Breathers; Opening Night Soprano Monsarat Caballe and Flutist Ransom Wilson Compare Notes on How They Support Their Sounds," _Opera News_, 45 (Sept 1980):42-44.

G. Music and Other Arts

Brody, E. and Fowkes, R. T. The German Lied and its Poetry. New York: New York University Press, 1971.

Brown, Calvin. Music and Literature; A Comparison of the Arts. Athens, Georgia: The University of Georgia Press, 1948.

Ferguson, Donald. Music as Metaphor. The Elements of Expression. Minneapolis: University of Minnesota Press, 1960.

Hollander, John. The Untuning of the Sky. Ideas of Music in English Poetry, 1500-1700. Princeton: Princeton University Press, 1961.

Ivey, Donald. Song: Anatomy, Imagery and Style. New York: The Free Press, 1970.

Lockspeiser, Edward. Music and Painting. A Study in Comparative Ideas From Turner to Schoenberg. New York: Harper and Row, Publishers, 1973

Mellers, Wilfred. Harmonious Meeting; A Study of Music, Poetry and Theatre in England, 1600-1900. London: Dennis Dobson, 1965.

Scher, Steven Paul. Verbal Music in German Literature. New Haven: Yale University Press, 1968.

Schmidgall, Gary. Literature as Opera. New York: Oxford University Press, 1977.

Stein, Jack. Poem and Music in the German Lied From Gluck to Hugo Wolf. Cambridge: Harvard University Press, 1971.

Thomas, R. Hinton. Poetry and Song in the German Baroque. A Study of the Continuo Lied. Oxford: Clarendon Press, 1963.

Winn, James Anderson. Unsuspected Eloquence: A History of the Relations between Poetry & Music. New Haven & London: Yale University Press, 1981.

CHAPTER IV

AUDIO MATERIAL

A.   Accompaniments Unlimited

Accompaniments Unlimited
P. O. Box36163
Grosse Pointe Branch
Grosse Pointe, Michigan 48236

As far as I can tell, each tape comes with only one song, at a cost ranging from $4.95 to $6.45. I was not supplied with any information that indicates otherwise. Choices are varied but tend toward the more popular. The catalogue sent me was copyright 1972, the revised price list dated 1978.

B.   Cassette Coach

Cassette Coach and Custom Cassette Coach
Elena Enterprises Inc.
48 South Evanston Way
Aurora, Colorado 80012

Cassette Coach offers seven tapes of arias, each tape providing an explanation of the aria's context within the opera, a slow reading of the text followed by an English translation, performance suggestions and professional accompaniment. Each tape has six arias and each costs $38.75 plus postage and handling. Available tapes are:

                    Puccini Arias for Soprano
                    Mozart Arias for Soprano
                    Favorite Soprano Arias
                    Favorite Tenor Arias
                    Arias for Mezzo-Soprano
                    Arias for Baritone
                    Arias for Bass

Custom Cassette Coach provides tapes individually produced with whatever material the student requests. Accompaniments alone, or with a reading of foreign texts if desired. Cost is determined by length of tape.

C.   Educo Records

Educo Records
P. O. Box 3006
Ventura, California 93003

       Educo has records of accompaniments only, as well as other records
of value to the voice teacher.   Prices vary depending on the number of records
purchased and whether or not payment is enclosed.   The range is from $6.22 (if
12 records are purchased, check enclosed) to $7.95 each, if they do the billing.
The accompaniment only records are:

               Songs you love to sing
               Robert Schumann: Liederkreis, op. 39, and others (I assume
                    in original key)
               Robert Schumann: Dichterliebe, and others
               Anthology of Italian Song, high and low voice
               Anthology of Modern French Song
               Favorite songs of Brahms, Wolf, and Strauss
               Schubert: Die Schöne Müllerin and other songs (Two-record
                    set, I assume in original key.)
               Debussy: Songs for voice and piano, high and low voice
               Songs for women: Schubert and Schumann (Frauenliebe und
                    Leben)
               More songs for women: Schubert, Brahms (Eight Gypsy Songs),
                    deFalla (Seven Spanish Folk Songs)
               Songs for men: Wolf and Brahms (Four Serious Songs)
               More songs for men: Mussorgsky (Songs and Dances of Death),
                    Beethoven and Handel
               Operatic arias for mezzo-soprano or alto. Four arias sung
                    by Julia Araya on one side, piano accompaniment only
                    on the other side.
               More operatic arias for mezzo-soprano or alto. Four different
                    arias sung by Julia Araya on one side, piano accompani-
                    ment only on the other.
               Schubert: Die Winterreise (Two-record set, looks like
                    medium voice).
               Songs by Franz Schubert
               Favorite tenor arias. Eleven arias of Mozart, Verdi, Donizetti,
                    Puccini, von Flotow, Massenet and Bizet.
               Puccini: Favorite arias for soprano
               Puccini: More favorite arias for soprano
               Wagner (Wesendonck Lieder) and Mahler (Songs of a Wayfarer),
                    high voice
               Songs of Poulenc, original key (Le Bestiaire, Fetes Galantes,
                    Chansons Gaillardes, Banalites, Airs Chantes
               Songs of Beethoven, high voice: includes the cycle An die
                    ferne Geliebte.
               Mozart songs, high voice
               Favorite baritone arias. Eight arias by Mozart, Gounod,
                    Massenet, Wagner, Verdi, and Leoncavallo.
               Two centuries of American song
               Spanish songs
               Bergerettes: Twenty melodies, accompaniment only on side one,
                    with the verses spoken in French on side two. Music
                    is available separately.

D.   Music Minus One

Music Minus One
Belwin Mills, Exclusive Distributor
Melville, New York   11747

        On long-playing records, $10.98 each.   They used to provide the
music for the missing instrument or voice, but no mention was made in the
catalogue.   Also, the catalogue provides no break-down of what is on each
record.

                    Schubert songs, volume one, high and low voice
                    Schubert songs, volume two, high and low voice
                    Brahms songs, low voice
                    Favorite songs, volume one, high voice and low voice
                    Favorite songs, volume two, high and low voice
                    Soprano Opera Arias
                    Mezzo Opera Arias
                    Tenor Opera Arias
                    Baritone Opera Arias
                    Bass Opera Arias
                    Hugo Wolf songs, high voice
                    Richard Strauss songs, high voice
                    Sacred Oratorio Arias, soprano
                    Sacred Oratorio Arias, tenor
                    Sacred Oratorio Arias, Bass
                    Schumann songs for high voice
                    Schumann songs for low voice
                    Verdi Arias for soprano
                    French Opera Arias for soprano
                    Contest solos intermediate, soprano
                    Contest solos beginning, mezzo-soprano
                    Contest solos intermediate, mezzo-soprano
                    Contest solos advanced, mezzo-soprano
                    Contest solos beginning, alto
                    Contest solos beginning, tenor
                    Contest solos advanced, tenor

        E.   Pocket Coach Publications

Pocket Coach Publications
Dietrich Erbelding, Producer and Publisher
31 Pamaron Way, Dept. UB
Novato, California 94947

        Each tape has 6 to 8 songs, all tapes are available in high or low
voice, and word for word translations are provided.   In addition, each poem
is read in its entirety for flow, then in short phrases with pauses for correct
pronunciation, then spoken rhythmically over the melody.   Currently, each tape
is $14.95, except the Italian Art-Song series which is $36 for three tapes when
all are purchased together.
        Future tapes will include all six roles of "Cosi fan Tutte", and ten
Lieder cycles.

Tapes now available are:

Six songs of Mozart
Six songs of Schumann
Seven songs of Richard Strauss
Eight songs of Schubert
Eight songs of Wolf
Eight songs of Brahms
Italian Art-Song Series. Three tapes which include all
    24 of the Schirmer "24 Italian Songs and Arias."
Mozart Arias for the young soprano. Other tapes of
    Mozart arias to be released in the future.
Handel: Messiah arias. Tape 1 women, tape 2 men.
Selected English arias, high voice
Schubert's Winterreise in original key. Three tapes
    with binder $40.
Schumann's Frauenliebe und Leben available in high
    or low voice.
Schumann's Der Arme Peter available in high or low
    voice, $12.95.
Translations of the Lieder are available by purchasing
    Paquin's book, Ten Cycles of Lieder for $15.

F. Song Study Series

Song Study Series
Belwin Mills, Exclusive Distributor
Melville, New York 11747

An extensive list of available cassettes of accompaniments,
each costing $9.95 at this writing:

24 Italian Songs and Arias, volume one, high and low
    voice
24 Italian Songs and Arias, volume two, high and low
    voice
50 Songs from the Modern Repertoire (a total of sixteen
    songs from that collection)
20th Century Art Songs for medium voice (sixteen songs)
Purcell songs for high voice (13 songs)
Purcell songs for low voice (13 songs, but not all are
    the same as high voice)
Menotti: Canti delli lontananza, and Argento: Six
    Elizabethan songs, high voice
The Young Singer, soprano (18 songs from that collection)
The Young Singer, mezzo soprano (18 songs from that
    collection)
The Young Singer, tenor (17 songs from that collection)
The Young Singer, bariton (17 songs from that collection)
Russian songs for high voice

Mozart: Exultate, Jubilate, and works by Rossini and
    Vivaldi, high voice
Berger: 4 songs (poems by Langston Hughes),
    Persichetti: Emily Dickinson Songs,
    Crist: Chinese Mother Goose Rhymes,
    Riete: Two Songs Between Two Waltzes, medium
    voice
Mahler songs for high voice (Lieder eines fahrenden
    Gesellen and songs from Des Knaben Wunderhorn)
Mahler songs for low voice (songs are same as above)
Beethoven songs for high voice (includes An die ferne
    Geliebte)
Beethoven songs for low voice
Chausson songs for high voice (Poeme de l'amour et de
    la mer)
Debussy songs for high voice (includes Fêtes Galantes
    and Chanson de Bilitis)
Debussy songs for low voice (same as above)
Debussy songs for high voice, volume two (Ariettes
    Oubliees)
Debussy songs for low voice, volume two (same as above)
Faure songs for high voice
Faure songs for low voice
Duparc songs for high voice
Duparc songs for low voice
Bach solo cantata (Ich habe genug), Mussorgsky (Without
    Sun), Barber (Dover Beach), baritone
Handel arias for soprano
Handel arias for alto
Handel arias for tenor
Handel arias for bass
Songs of Prokofieff, Honegger and Chausson, high voice
Poulenc songs (Tel jour, telle nuit, Airs Chantes,
    Cinq Poemes de Paul Eluard), high voice
Ravel songs (Chansons Madecasses, Don Quichotte, Cinq
    Melodies Populaires Grecques), medium voice
Barber songs for high and low voice
Respighi songs for medium voice
Vaughan Williams (Songs of Travel), Quilter (Five
    Elizabethan Songs and Three Elizabethan Songs),
    high voice
Same as above for low voice
Schubert songs, volume one, for high and low voice
Schubert (Schwanengesang), high and low voice
Schumann songs, volume one (Dichterliebe), high and
    low voice
Schumann songs, volume two, high and low voice
Operatic arias for soprano, volume one
Operatic arias for mezzo-soprano, volume one
Operatic arias for tenor, volume one
Operatic arias for baritone, volume one
Operatic arias for bass, volume one

177

G. Singer's Pronunciation Guide

The Walden Group
P. O. Box 225
Hastings on Hudson, New York 10706

  Conceived and directed by Arthur Liet, each cassette ($13.50)
includes texts read slowly by a native-language teacher, and a printed
booklet of original texts with word-for-word English translations.

    Italian Classic Airs (59 texts)
    Schubert Lider (31 texts)
    French Art Songs (30 texts)

All three for $35.00

SONG TITLES

The songs are here listed alphabetically, with the number representing the
entry number in the main body of the book. Foreign languages are indicated: g = German; it = Italian; fr = French; e = English; la = Latin;
no = Norwegian. If no language is indicated, the song is in English only.

185

187

188

190

COMPOSERS